WHAT YOU NEED TO KNOW ABOUT

ECONOMICS

GEORGE BUCKLEY & SUMEET DESAI

CAPSTONE

D0111671

This edition first published 2011
© 2011 George Buckley and Sumeet Desai

Registered office
Capstone Publishing Ltd. (A Wiley Company), The Atrium, Southern
Gate, Chichester, West Sussex, PO19 8SQ, United Kingdom

For details of our global editorial offices, for customer services and for
information about how to apply for permission to reuse the copyright
material in this book please see our website at www.wiley.com.

The right of the author to be identified as the author of this work has
been asserted in accordance with the Copyright, Designs and Patents Act
1988.

All rights reserved. No part of this publication may be reproduced,
stored in a retrieval system, or transmitted, in any form or by any means,
electronic, mechanical, photocopying, recording or otherwise, except as
permitted by the UK Copyright, Designs and Patents Act 1988, without
the prior permission of the publisher.

Wiley also publishes its books in a variety of electronic formats. Some
content that appears in print may not be available in electronic books.

Designations used by companies to distinguish their products are often
claimed as trademarks. All brand names and product names used in
this book are trade names, service marks, trademarks or registered
trademarks of their respective owners. The publisher is not associated
with any product or vendor mentioned in this book. This publication
is designed to provide accurate and authoritative information in regard
to the subject matter covered. It is sold on the understanding that
the publisher is not engaged in rendering professional services. If
professional advice or other expert assistance is required, the services
of a competent professional should be sought.

Library of Congress Cataloguing-in-Publication Data

9780857081148 (paperback), 9780857081223 (ebook),
9780857081254 (epub), 9780857081261 (emobi)

A catalogue record for this book is available from the British Library.

Set in 10.5 pt New Baskerville by Toppan Best-set Premedia Limited

Printed and Bound in the United Kingdom by TJ International, Padstow,
Cornwall.

This is the stuff you've always been embarrassed to ask about the world of modern business.

That *What You Need to Know ...* books can get you up to speed on a core business subject fast. Whether it's for a new job, a new responsibility, or a meeting with someone you need to impress, these books will give you what you need to get by from someone who knows what they're talking about.

Each book contains:

- ▶ **What It's all About** – A summary of key points
- ▶ **Who You Need to Know** – The basics about the key players
- ▶ **Who Said It** – Quotes from key figures
- ▶ **What You Need to Read** – Books and online resources for if you want to deepen your knowledge
- ▶ **How You Need to Do It** – Key tips for using the knowledge
- ▶ **If You Only Remember One Thing** – A one-liner of the most important information

You might also want to know:

- ▶ *What You Need to Know about Business*
- ▶ *What You Need to Know about Project Management*
- ▶ *What You Need to Know about Strategy*
- ▶ *What You Need to Know about Leadership*
- ▶ *What You Need to Know about Marketing*
- ▶ *What You Need to Know about Starting a Business*

CONTENTS

INTRODUCTION

Have you ever wondered what makes an economy tick, and why recessions happen? Or why prices rise and fall? Why do governments borrow money, and why does it matter if they borrow too much? What causes unemployment? Why are house prices so important for the economy? And what is it that causes our savings rates and the cost of borrowing to move up and down?

If you have, then you're already interested in economics.

These are the sort of issues that we hear about every day in the newspapers and on the television news. There's always been a certain fascination with what's going on in the economy. This has been particularly true since the global credit crisis, with the recession that followed having had such as large impact on economies and businesses worldwide.

Never has it been more important to understand what's going on in the world of economics. The last few years have shown us that we can't always rely on strong economic growth and a rate of inflation that remains stable from one year to the next. Sometimes things go wrong, and when they do the economy is rarely out of the news.

To the uninitiated, understanding economics can be a daunting prospect. Sometimes news stories assume that the reader, viewer or listener knows more about economics than is actually the case. But you don't need a degree to understand economics. In fact, economics is a very logical subject and the basics can be grasped very easily. It is no coincidence that the eighteenth century economist Adam Smith – dubbed the Father of Economics – began his career at Glasgow University as Professor of Logic.

What this book aims to do is to provide a basic introduction to the subject of economics. Understanding economics is one of the cornerstones of running any business. So having a feel for what's going on in the economy will give you a much better idea of the factors that are driving your business – both now and in the future.

Whether you're in business and want to have a better feel for the economic forces that are affecting your bottom line, or you're just looking to improve your general awareness of how the economy works, then this book provides a simple introduction to the subject. It explains key economic ideas in simple terms, and we hope it will whet your appetite for reading more about the subject of economics in the future.

So, in summary, if you're after an introduction to the broad field of economics then you need look no further than this book. Economics is a fascinating subject, one which is becoming ever more popular within schools and universities up and down the country. Take a look in your local bookshop and you'll see how much interest there is by the number of books on popular economics and, in particular, the recent credit crisis.

This book gives you the resources you need to get a clearer picture of how the economy works, what economic developments mean for you and your business, and an ability to better understand the economic analysis and discussion you read in the newspapers and see on television every day.

CHAPTER 1
GROWTH

WHAT IT'S ALL ABOUT

- ► How to measure the size of the economy and how fast it's growing
- ► How flows of money move around the economy
- ► How people's incomes affect their decisions about spending or saving
- ► How activity moves up and down but generally rises over time
- ► Why a rise in spending can have a magnified effect on the economy
- ► What recessions are and why they happen

WHAT IS ECONOMIC GROWTH?

We hear regularly on the TV and radio news, and in newspapers and online, about how quickly the economy is expanding or – as has been the case during the financial crisis – contracting. But what exactly is this thing we call 'the economy', and how do we measure its size and rate of growth?

The size of the economy is often referred to as GDP – which stands for 'Gross Domestic Product'. One way to measure the size of the economy is to add up the total amount (Gross) in a country (Domestic) of all the goods & services made (Product). This is called the *output* measure of GDP, but there are two other ways we can get to this number. We can add up the total amount that we *spend* on goods & services. Or we can measure economic activity by looking at the total amount of *income* that has been earned.

We usually measure economic activity over a period of three months – a 'quarter' – or over an entire year. The rate of economic growth is then simply the percentage change in GDP from one quarter to the next (the quarterly growth rate), or from one quarter to the same period a year later (annual growth). Sometimes, the quarterly growth rate is shown as an 'annualised' figure – in other words, how quickly the economy would grow over an entire year if it continued at the rate achieved during that one quarter.

Growth in the US and Europe over the past 30 years

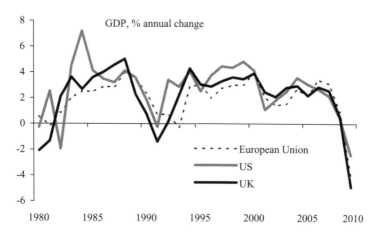

GDP, % annual change

THREE MEASURES OF ACTIVITY

The three measures of GDP, or economic activity, outlined above should be identical, in theory at least, because any *income* earned is then *spent* on the goods & services that have been *produced*. In practice, however, it is difficult to measure economic activity precisely so getting the three measures to equal one another can be difficult. Let's take a closer look at these different ways of working out the size of economy.

1. Output

The output measure adds up the value of all goods & services produced in the economy. This includes

7

the output of manufacturing, mining and energy
supply companies – collectively called 'industrial production' – as well as construction and agricultural
output.

It also includes the output of the service industries,
even though they do not make physical products like
manufacturers do. These include transport and telecom-
munications firms, restaurants, hotels, banks, account-
ants and estate agents to name but a few – all of
which provide valuable services to the economy. In developed economies such as the UK, US and Europe, the
service sector has become much more important in
recent years, while the manufacturing base has become
ever smaller.

Shifts in the structure of the UK economy

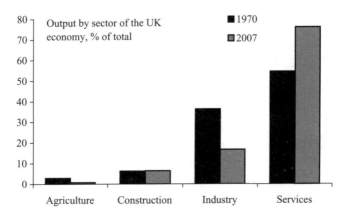

2. Income

We can measure GDP by adding together how much is earned across the economy. This means adding together wages paid to workers, rent paid to land owners and profits paid to the owners of firms. You may sometimes hear these three key inputs – labour, land and capital – referred to as the 'factors of production'. This is because they are the three basic components, combined together with technological know-how, required when we produce goods & services.

3. Spending

Most importantly, let's turn to the spending measure of GDP. If we were to measure the size of the economy by looking at everyone's outgoings we would need to think not just about how much we spend as individuals, but spending by other groups too. Investment spending by firms, for example, must be included. We often think of investment as the purchase by a firm of buildings and machines, but we must not forget that when firms change their stocks (or inventories) that is also a type of investment because they can be stored and sold at a later date. Governments spend money on goods & services – both current expenditure and for investment purposes – which is also a part of GDP. It is worth noting that we do not include benefit payments like jobseekers' allowance – these will already be included in how much *individuals* receive from the government which they may then go on to spend, so to include it would be double counting. Finally, we also add in how much is spent by people abroad on our exports, less the amount we spend on imports from abroad (as the latter represents an outflow of money from the economy).

So, in summary total spending in the economy is made up of:

▶ how much households spend;
▶ investment by firms (including stock-building);
▶ spending by the government;
▶ spending on exports (less imports).

HOW IT ALL FITS TOGETHER

The interaction between these groups – households, firms, the government and the international sector – in an economy is called the 'circular flow of income', and getting a flavour of this helps us understand how economies work. Put simply, firms produce goods & services and pay their employees an income for doing so. Firms also pay rent to landowners while the profits go to the firms' owners. Households then use some of that income up by spending it on the goods & services produced by firms – which is why it is called the *circular* flow of income. The best way to show all of this is in the diagram on page 12.

As you can see, it is not *quite* as simple as that. As income moves round this circular system, some money is removed, but at the same time some money is injected back in. Money can be removed in three ways: (i) by spending on imports (as the money goes abroad), (ii) paying taxes to the government, and (iii) saving money in banks and other financial institutions. Additions of money come about in similar but conceptually opposite ways: (i) people abroad spending money on our exports, (ii) the government spending taxpayers' money on public services, and (iii) firms borrowing people's savings from banks to invest.

When the amount of cash that leaves the circular flow (imports, taxes, savings) is the same as the cash that enters the system (exports, government spending and investment) then we have some sort of happy balance – or, as economists call it, 'equilibrium'. When they don't match up this can cause either the economy to run too fast (additions higher than withdrawals) or alternatively too slow (withdrawals higher than additions).

In the diagram overleaf, the grey circles are the various groups or 'sectors' in the economy, while the white circles show the markets for jobs as well as goods & services. The arrows refer to money flows – the red ones represent money removed from the system, the blue ones money added back in. Take some time to look at this diagram and it should become clear how it all fits together. In particular, it helps to explain why the output, income and spending measures of GDP should all be the same – because they are just measuring the flow of money at

The circular flow of income

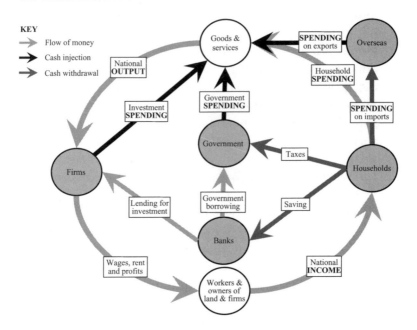

KEY
→ Flow of money
→ Cash injection
→ Cash withdrawal

Goods & services

SPENDING on exports

Overseas

National **OUTPUT**

Household **SPENDING**

Investment **SPENDING**

Government **SPENDING**

SPENDING on imports

Government

Taxes

Firms

Lending for investment

Government borrowing

Saving

Households

Banks

Wages, rent and profits

National **INCOME**

Workers & owners of land & firms

WHO SAID IT

An individual is "led by an invisible hand to promote an end which was no part of his intention ... By pursuing his own interest he frequently promotes that of the society more effectually than when he really intends to promote it."
– **Adam Smith**

different points in the circle (the three measures are shown in capital letters in the diagram above to make them easier to spot).

FOCUS ON HOUSEHOLD SPENDING AND INVESTMENT BY FIRMS

Let's think about the spending measure of GDP. We take a more detailed look at government spending and international trade (exports and imports) later on in the book, so for now let's focus on the main factors influencing spending by households and firms.

What UK households spend money on

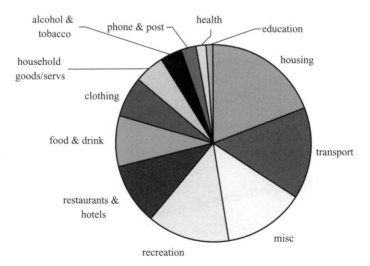

Household spending is one of the most important components of total expenditure because it is worth such a large portion of the economy. In fact, in many advanced economies around two thirds of all spending is done by households. The previous chart shows what we spend our money on in the UK. Close to half of it goes on what we might term necessities – things like housing, transport, food and drink, health and education – which probably does not change that much from one year to the next.

When we choose what portion of our income to spend, we must also make a simultaneous decision about what portion of income we want to save. This is called the household saving ratio and is shown in the chart below for the UK.

Movements in the UK household saving ratio over time

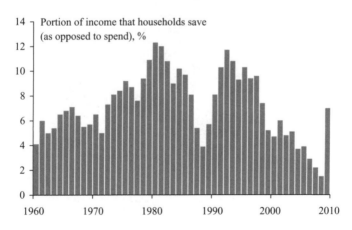

Portion of income that households save (as opposed to spend), %

Over the years there has been a lot of important work done to investigate how households decide how much to spend and save at any point in time. There are lots of things that will affect this decision, including interest rates, for example (higher rates dissuade spending because it is more costly to borrow, and encourage saving because of higher returns). Even the value of our homes or the shares we might own could affect how much we spend – the more wealthy we feel, the more likely we are to buy things. This is called the 'wealth effect'.

Leaving these influences aside, one of the biggest debates among economists in the past has been about how the *level of income* affects spending. Back in the 1930s, John Maynard Keynes – one of the most important economists of all time – argued that the amount of money people spend would depend mainly on how much they *currently* earn in their job.

While that might sound reasonable, it seemed too crude to Milton Friedman, an American Nobel Prize winning economist who looked into these issues back in the 1950s and 1960s. He argued that how much people will spend depends not only on their current earnings, but also on how much they think they will earn in the future – something he called 'permanent income'.

This is an important conclusion for two reasons. Firstly, because it means that people will *smooth* their spending over time. In years where a person's earnings have been especially good they may squirrel more of it away, so they

WHO YOU NEED TO KNOW
John Maynard Keynes

John Maynard Keynes was one of the most influential economic thinkers of the twentieth century. Keynes devoted his time looking at a branch of economics called *macroeconomics* – the study of how the economy operates as a whole. In his work published between the two world wars (the most important of which was *The General Theory of Employment, Interest and Money*, 1936) he looked at the factors that determined key economic variables such as interest rates, inflation, output and unemployment.

He argued a key driver of economic activity was the difference between how much people want to save and how much firms want to invest. Unlike the views of his predecessors (the 'classical' economists such as Adam Smith), Keynes believed interest rates would not always be at a level that would equilibrate the two. Too *much* saving would mean not enough spending, which in turn could cause recession. While too *little* saving could cause a boom in consumer spending and in turn lead to higher inflation.

Keynes was a firm believer in intervention by the central bank and the government. Leaving the economy to its own devices (a policy known as 'laissez faire') may mean a prolonged period of too much or too little activity. By changing interest rates and public spending/taxes, economic activity and inflation could be managed by the authorities over a shorter period. He even went as far as to say that if total, or 'aggregate' as economists call it, demand in the economy was too low (and unemployment too high), governments could help by burying banknotes in bottles which people would then dig up and spend! To be a 'Keynesian', therefore, means to support government intervention in the economy through a process of 'demand management'.

can draw upon it in bad years when their income may be lower. Someone who is worried about losing their job, for example, might opt to save more now so that they have savings to see them through their period of expected unemployment. Secondly, it means that government intervention – such as tax cuts – may not have the desired effect to support the economy. The reason is that people may not spend all of their extra disposable income if they think the government will only end up raising taxes again in the future.

The economic data shows this smoothing of consumer spending to be true – the amount households spend is not only one of the largest but also one of the *least variable* components of total spending in the economy. Economists call the proportion of income that people spend – as opposed to save – the 'propensity to consume', which for both individuals and society as a whole will depend on income distribution. For example, people who are less well off tend to spend a greater portion of their income than richer people do.

The relative stability we see in consumption is not the case when we look at how much businesses invest, however. Investment is usually a smaller part of total spending than consumption, but it can change quite quickly. Keynes said this was due to the 'animal spirits' of investors. As a result, investment swings can have a large effect on the rate at which the overall economy grows – both on the upside during the boom and on the downside during recessions.

How do firms decide how much to invest? If firms can't keep up with the amount of demand there is for their product, then they probably need to invest so they can produce more. On the other hand, if they are producing too much relative to what is required then they may need to invest less – or even retire some of their existing plant or machinery. In this case we say the firm has 'spare' or 'excess' capacity.

The cost of increasing the workforce must be accounted for, because more machinery will likely mean more people required to operate it. And the price of what the firm sells compared with the cost of investing – the interest rate – will be an important consideration too. Unlike Keynes, classical economists believed that interest rates in the market should, without intervention, eventually move to a level whereby households will want save as much as firms desire to invest.

VOLUMES, VALUES AND THE SEASONS

Before we begin to look at economic cycles, there are two more things that are important to know about GDP.

First, this may sound obvious but the size of the economy will vary depending on the time of year. For example, economic activity is usually higher from October to December than it is during any other quarter of the year as production, spending, and income are all raised for Christmas. Distortions such as this can make it difficult to analyse the underlying trend in the economy, so we usually adjust GDP for such seasonal influences. That way, if adjusted output rises strongly towards the end of the year we can be sure it is because of something else other than the usual Christmas effect.

The second issue relates to prices. So far, you might have assumed that we've been talking about GDP in cash, or 'nominal', terms – in other words, the *value* of output produced or bought, or income earned. But normally when we hear about economic activity it is in 'real' terms – the *number* of goods produced or bought, or how many can be bought with the income we earn.

Consider the following example. Imagine the economy only produces handbags, and 100 are sold in the first year at a price of £10 each. In the following year, let's say the same number is sold, but the price has risen to £15 each. *Nominal GDP* in this case would have risen by 50% from £1000 to £1500 between the two years, but *real GDP* – the amount physically produced in the economy – would be unchanged.

There will be occasions when we prefer to look at nominal instead of real activity, but generally speaking when we talk about the growth rate of an economy we are refer-ring to the volume of (or real) GDP.

BUSINESS CYCLES AND TREND GROWTH

As we have seen, the rate at which the economy grows can vary considerably over time. Sometimes activity growth is strong, sometimes it is weak, and on occasion activity actually contracts, as it did sharply in many developed countries during the recent financial crisis. This process of ups and downs in GDP around a generally rising trend is referred to by economists as the 'business cycle'.

The business cycle

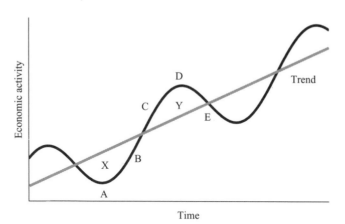

Let's examine the phases of a normal business cycle using the graph above, starting at point A. This is pretty much where many advanced economies stood immediately after the recession of 2008–09. Activity in most countries had stabilised after falling sharply during the banking sector crisis, reflected in the line flattening out.

Following a recession, the next stage of a typical economic cycle is recovery, indicated by points B and C. Economic activity at first begins to increase slowly before speeding up (point B) as it bounds back from its recession-lows (it's worth just reminding ourselves here that the line in the graph above shows the *level* of activity – so the steeper the line, the faster the rate of growth).

As the economy continues to grow, probably supported by the central bank and the government (interest rates and taxes will likely have been lowered, while government spending should be higher too), activity eventually moves back above its trend level (point C). The growth rate here is becoming faster – probably because of something known as the 'accelerator theory'. As GDP recovers so too do firms' profits, in turn leading to greater investment, employment and incomes. Some of that income is then spent on goods & services, which feeds back into greater profits and the process continues.

A good way to understand the accelerator is to think about a football team. As the team's performance improves it moves into a higher league. The team then receives more money which can be spent on better players. That improves performance, resulting in a higher league position, more money and (once again) better players.

Returning to our cycle, after a while growth in economic activity will probably slow. Bottlenecks will be reached as firms simply can't supply goods & services to the economy as quickly as they are being demanded. It takes time for the investment that firms may be making at this point to raise their output – after all, factories can't be built over-night. Firms here are operating above their trend or potential level. At some point, the economy will stop growing (shown by a flattening of the activity line at point D) and a recession will follow again (point E), completing the cycle.

All of this is an over-generalisation, of course. Not all industries will experience the same ups and downs as the cycle as a whole – some will probably be relatively immune from such movements (such as electricity producers, for example, because people don't tend to change their spending on necessities like energy as much as they would the purchase of luxury goods, like handbags, over the cycle). And, in some countries more than others, politics influences the cycle as the government may raise spending ahead of an election to try to win over voters. In reality, every cycle is different.

MULTIPLIERS

No discussion of the business cycle would be complete without mention of what are known as 'multipliers'. The concept is simple – a rise in, say, investment or government spending will eventually trigger a larger rise in overall GDP than the initial increase in spending.

To explain, let's think about a real life example that happened during the most recent recession. Household spending on cars was badly hit in the 2008–09 recession – such discretionary spending tends to suffer disproportionately when there is economic uncertainty and tighter lending standards. In response, governments in a number of countries opted to support their car industries by introducing schemes encouraging people to buy new vehicles. In the UK it was called the 'car scrappage' scheme, in the US it was 'cash for clunkers'.

The UK scheme gave people £2000 towards a new car if they traded-in one which was over 10 years old, at a cost to the government of £400 million. Relative to the size of the economy this is not a particularly large sum of money – it amounted to just 0.03% of 2009 GDP, and even as a proportion of the total amount that people spent on cars in 2009 it was only worth 1%. However, the impact it had was much bigger. With more cars bought than would otherwise have been the case, more people were employed in the production process.

Those people then spent a portion of their incomes on other goods & services which they would otherwise have not been able to do had they been laid off. On top of that, think of all of the support industries that may have been bankrupted had car production not have been helped – windscreen glass makers, tyre manufacturers, light bulb factories – and in turn the firms that supply them. The importance of the multiplier effect will depend on the proportion of any extra income received that individuals spend – the higher it is, the more powerful the effect.

It is hardly surprising, then, why Keynes pushed the case for government intervention. If the economy is performing badly, then a dose of government spending should help as it adds more to activity than the amount originally spent. As with all things in economics, however, the argument for intervention is far from one-sided, as the rise in government borrowing can cause problems of its own and the money will eventually have to be paid back.

SPARE CAPACITY AND THE 'OUTPUT GAP'

Spare capacity is a key concept in economics. A manufacturer, for example, would be said to have spare capacity if running its plant at full speed led to over-production relative to what is required. Normally in these conditions a firm would scale back its output by keeping some of its machines idle or even closing plants entirely, laying off some of its workers and asking others to work fewer hours.

At the whole-economy level, spare capacity means that firms in aggregate are able to supply more goods & services than what is being demanded in the economy.

But how can we measure spare capacity? One way might be to look at the unemployment rate, as that tends to rise during periods of spare capacity.

But there is another way we can estimate spare capacity, and that is to calculate what is called an 'output gap' (something that is also referred to as an 'inflationary' or 'deflationary' gap). The easiest way to explain this is to go back to the graph on page 21, which showed the level of economic activity plotted against a trend. Think of this trend as the level of output that *could be* produced without generating inflation. The output gap is then just the difference between actual economic activity (the wavy line) and the trend or potential level of GDP (the grey straight line), normally expressed as a percentage.

An example will help here. Going back to our handbag manufacturer from earlier, if demand is weak and a firm is producing 90 handbags but has the ability to produce 100, then we would have a negative output (or *deflationary*) gap of 10% – area X in the graph on page 21. Alternatively, if demand is so strong that the firm produces 110 handbags by overworking its machines and its staff, then we would say there is a positive output (or *inflationary*) gap of 10% – area Y in the graph on page 21.

Why is this important? The degree of spare capacity can have consequences for inflation and thereby the level of interest rates that the central bank sets. However, estimating output gaps can be complicated because we don't know what trend or potential GDP actually is. Let's now

WHO YOU NEED TO KNOW
Joseph Schumpeter

Like Keynes, Joseph Schumpeter spent much of his time trying to understand the ups and downs of the business cycle although from a somewhat different perspective. He categorised three types of cycle: short ones, which last a year or two and are caused by firms adjusting their stock – or inventory – levels; medium-term ones lasting around a decade such as the ones we discuss in graph on page 21, which are the result of changes in firms' investment decisions; and much longer ones lasting many decades, which can be explained by waves of innovation. Examples of the latter include the Industrial Revolution, or perhaps the advent of the internet more recently.

The theory most associated with Schumpeter is that of 'creative destruction'. Firms continually introduce new and better products, or more efficient ways of producing their output, with the innovating firm reaping the profits and others attempting to copy it. The businesses that really suffer, however,

27

are the ones that fail to adapt to the new technology or more efficient means of production – they are destroyed by the introduction of these new and superior ways of doing business. A great example of this is the newspaper industry, where printing presses are being rapidly replaced by the internet.

turn to a specific part of the business cycle, where activity falls and moves below its trend level, in turn causing spare capacity. We call these periods recessions and, if bad enough, depressions.

RECESSIONS AND DEPRESSIONS

What is a recession? To be very general, it is when the economy contracts for a period of time. There may be occasions, however, when economic activity falls over a very short period because of some unusual event, then continues rising thereafter. This is not really the spirit of a recession, so we need a better way to define one than simply any time that activity falls. One definition might be when activity falls over the course of a year – just like the recessions that can be seen in the chart on page 7. The most common definition of a recession, however, is when GDP falls for *two* quarters back to back (in other words over a six-month period) – if this happens then it is difficult to dismiss it as being due to an unusual one-off event.

Still, some countries use different definitions. One of these is the United States, where the National Bureau of Economic Research (NBER) proclaims periods of recession based on a host of important economic indicators, not just activity. As the NBER explains: 'A recession is a significant decline in economic activity spread across the economy, lasting more than a few months, normally visible in real GDP, real income, employment, industrial production, and wholesale-retail sales'.

It is worth noting that while these definitions are true for any one country, they are not appropriate for the world as a whole. When we look at the global economy, because we are averaging across a lot of countries the good performers often offset the bad. As such, it is very rare that total world activity declines in any one year. There is an unwritten rule of thumb, therefore, that annual world growth below 2% per year is considered a recession. Still, the 2009 recession was so bad (and, crucially, so synchronised) that world activity actually *did* decline, as the chart below shows.

How long do recessions normally last? Just as all economic cycles are different, so too are the periods of recession within those cycles. Economic expansion is the 'default mode' for economies – each year it is usually the case that activity is higher than the previous one, partly because the growing population is consuming and producing more, and partly because the existing population is becoming more productive.

While less common, periods of falling output and spending are still part of the typical business cycle. In the UK, for example, the most recent recessions (those of 2008–09, the early 1990s and the early 1980s) have each lasted just over a year. The reason that the economy continues

World economic growth since 1980

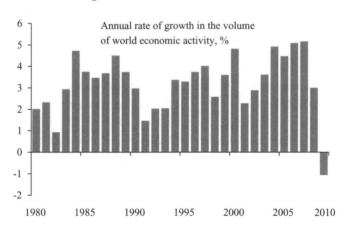

Annual rate of growth in the volume of world economic activity, %

Previous recessions in the UK

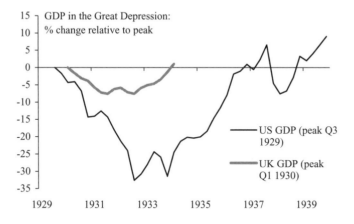

to feel weak for an extended period is because – as the graph on page 21 shows – it takes some time until the level of activity and employment returns back to its trend after output has stopped falling. In other words, the deflationary gap can remain negative for a long period after the recession even in the event of strong economic growth.

Some people use the terms 'recession' and 'depression' interchangeably. However, the term depression usually refers to a situation where the level of activity and employment not only falls sharply but subsequently fails to recover, remaining at low levels for a long time. To put it simply, a depression is a bad recession followed by a lacklustre recovery.

The graph above shows how the US and UK economies performed during the 1930s. While the UK experienced a deep recession (the level of activity fell by 7.5% from its peak to its trough, recovering reasonably quickly afterwards), the US went through a period of depression. Activity fell by more than 30% from peak to trough, and the economy suffered a double dip towards the end of the decade.

Japan's economy can also be described to have been in a state of depression for the last two decades. After experiencing a collapse in growth in the early 1990s, as the housing and stock market bubbles of the late 1980s burst, economic activity in nominal terms failed to recover – it stands at the same level now as it did almost 20 years ago.

Bubbles are a common precursor to recessions. In the good times the prices of assets such as houses and stocks get pushed too high as people lose track in the euphoria of what is the right value. People eventually realise, however, that prices have gone beyond their appropriate or fundamental levels, with the trigger for this often being a change in central bank or government policy (such as a rise in interest rates or taxes) or an external shock (such as oil price rises in the 1970s).

The last recession was no different. Homeowners in the US purchased housing beyond their means, taking out mortgages at exceptionally low interest rates and thereby bidding up house prices. But when interest rates rose they were left high and dry, unable to continue making their repayments. With banks globally holding these debts, a far reaching credit crisis resulted. Economies have become much more interlinked over the past few

WHO SAID IT

"If you owe your bank a hundred pounds, you
have a problem. But if you owe your bank
a million pounds, it has."
– **John Maynard Keynes**

decades, not only through international finance but also
trade. The result was a sharp and globally synchronised
downturn in economic activity, as the graph below shows.

Recessions in advanced countries during the credit crisis

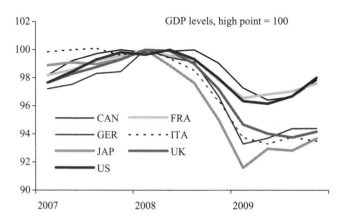

COMPARING ECONOMIES ACROSS THE WORLD

Which economies in the world have the highest activity? In terms of total GDP (in current US dollar terms), the US is the largest economy accounting for a total of just over 20% of world output. It is followed by China (12.5%), then Japan (6%), India (5%) and Germany (4%). The UK, Russia, France and Brazil come next (each worth close to 3% of world GDP) then Italy (2.5%) and Mexico (2%). All other countries have GDP worth less than 2% of the world total.

When making international comparisons we shouldn't just look at total GDP – which tells us what size an economy is relative to others – but also GDP *per head*, which is a better (but not perfect) measure of living standards. For example, while China is a bigger economy than the UK, there are a lot more people living in China who must share that GDP. Qatar, Luxembourg and Norway are the richest three countries in terms of GDP per person, while Liberia, The Congo and Zimbabwe are the poorest three.

The following chart shows both measures of GDP across the G20 group of countries, alongside their world rankings (the observant among you will notice that there are only 19 countries in the G20).

While per head figures are useful for cross-country comparisons in any one year, they are not especially

Comparing the world's major economies

Country	Size (US $ per head)	Rank	Size (% of world GDP)	Rank
Argentina	14,561	53	0.8	23
Australia	38,911	11	1.2	18
Brazil	10,514	76	2.9	9
Canada	38,025	14	1.8	14
China	6,567	100	12.5	2
France	33,679	22	3.0	8
Germany	34,212	21	4.0	5
India	2,941	129	5.1	4
Indonesia	4,157	121	1.4	15
Italy	29,109	28	2.5	10
Japan	32,608	24	6.0	3
Mexico	13,628	61	2.1	11
Russia	14,920	52	3.0	7
Saudi Arabia	23,221	39	0.9	22
South Africa	10,244	78	0.7	25
South Korea	27,978	31	1.9	13
Turkey	12,476	66	1.2	16
UK	34,619	20	3.1	6
USA	46,381	6	20.5	1

helpful for analysing changes in GDP in a country over short periods of time for the obvious reason that population doesn't change very much from one quarter to the next.

WHAT TO WATCH

Let's put what we've learnt so far into practice and take a look at the information that is published about the size of the economy. The quickest countries to publish GDP do so in the month after the quarter to which the numbers relate. For example, GDP for the first quarter of the year (January to March) is published towards the end of April for both the UK and the US. European countries usually take a little longer. But they are all eclipsed by Singapore and China, both of which release their numbers within two weeks of quarter-end.

For many countries GDP is published so quickly that there is a lot of information missing. When the statistics office computes GDP it relies on company surveys, income and sales tax receipts, details of government spending – all of which take time to be returned. So with early estimates of GDP it's a case of trading data quality for timeliness of publication, as a good portion is based on guesstimates by the statistics office. It is perhaps not surprising, therefore, that GDP often gets revised substantially as more news is received over time about activity in any given quarter.

GDP news can have a significant impact on the financial markets. Interest rate expectations and share prices can move sharply in the event of an unexpectedly high or low economic growth reading. Economists usually have at least an idea of what the early estimate of GDP might look like because many of the components have already been released for some months of the quarter. On the spending side, monthly retail sales (a large portion of overall household spending), government expenditure and import/export data will have been reported for part of the period, while on the output side we know something about industrial production and service sector output. Still, GDP can be volatile and surprises are not uncommon.

WHAT YOU NEED TO READ

► The National Bureau of Economic Research (NBER) explains how it identifies recessions in the US here: *www.nber.org/cycles/recessions.html*.

► Statistics on growth rates around the world along with interesting research articles can be found on the International Monetary Fund's (IMF) website: *www.imf.org/external/data*.

► The UK statistics office webpage, which explains the practicalities of computing GDP, can be found here: *www.statistics.gov.uk/gdp*.

► A good introductory macroeconomics text book is Joseph G. Nellis and David Parker. *The Essence of the Economy*, Prentice Hall, 2006 (2nd edition).

► For a recent history of the UK economy, as told by the Chancellors of the Exchequer at the time, see Howard Davis, *The Chancellors' Tales*, Polity, 2006.

IF YOU ONLY REMEMBER ONE THING

The way that money flows around the economy means we can measure activity by looking at output, income or spending. Activity moves up and down during the course of the business cycle, causing periods of boom but also recessions.

CHAPTER 2
INFLATION

WHAT IT'S ALL ABOUT

- ▶ What inflation is and how it is measured
- ▶ How prices are determined by demand and supply
- ▶ How inflation can be caused by higher spending or rising costs
- ▶ Why both inflation and deflation can be bad for an economy
- ▶ The extremes of deflation and hyperinflation
- ▶ Why inflation expectations are important

WHAT IS INFLATION?

Pick up almost any economics textbook and you will find this definition of inflation: it is a rise in the general level of prices in an economy sustained over time. There are two words that are particularly important here – *general* and *sustained*. We use the word *general* to get across that we are not talking about a rise in the price of a single good or service, but of goods & services across the economy. Of course, some prices will inevitably go up and some down during a period of inflation. Movements in the prices of individual goods & services are referred to as changes in *relative* prices, but a period of inflation is when the trend in *general* prices is up. *Sustained* means that inflation is not a one off rise in the general price level, but a more persistent increase in prices.

Normally, when we talk about inflation, we are referring to the annual rate of increase in the prices that households face when buying goods & services in the shops or online. These are measured by the consumer price index (CPI) or the retail price index (RPI) in the UK. These are simply two different measures of inflation, with the biggest difference between them being that RPI includes housing costs and mortgage interest payments. CPI is the one the Bank of England looks at when targeting inflation.

Not only do households face inflation but so too do retailers themselves. They buy goods from manufacturers which they then sell on to households. The prices of the

Prices at different stages of the production and consumption process

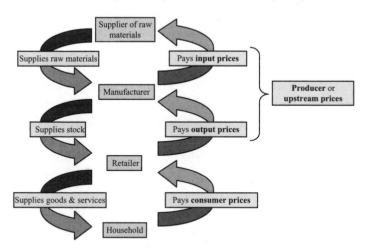

goods which the manufacturer sells to retailers are called 'output' prices. In turn, manufacturing firms must pay for the raw materials required to produce the products they sell to retailers. The prices of these goods are called 'input' prices or costs. Both input and output prices are collectively known as 'producer' (or 'upstream') prices, because they are the prices charged by producers.

The relationship between input prices, output prices and consumer prices is shown in the diagram above. The difference between output and input prices tells us something about manufacturers' margins or profits, while the difference between consumer and output prices reflects the retailer's margin. Although in both cases we mustn't forget to take into consideration other costs, like wages and overheads, when thinking about firms' profits.

Generally, when we talk about inflation in this and subsequent chapters we will be referring to the rate of growth of consumer prices, unless otherwise mentioned. But what sorts of thing are included in consumer prices?

To calculate inflation, the statistics office sends its researchers around the country each month to gather the prices of a 'basket' of goods & services that are intended to represent the purchases of a typical family. This basket is usually made up of twelve different components: food & drink, alcohol & tobacco, clothing & footwear, housing & energy, furniture & household goods, health, transport, communication, recreation, education, restaurants & hotels and miscellaneous items (the latter including the cost of financial services, such as insurance, and personal effects like jewellery).

While the components may be generally the same, the *importance* of each in the basket will be different across countries and will also change over time, reflecting the portion of an average household's spending that is devoted to those particular goods & services. For example, in the euro area the price of recreational goods & services in the CPI is worth around 10% of the total basket, while in the UK it is worth much more at 15%. Of course any given household in any given month will inevitably not buy the same goods & services that are in the basket,

The relative importance of the shopping basket: UK vs. Europe

	UK	Euro
Transport	16.4%	15.3%
Recreation & culture	15.0%	9.7%
Housing & energy	12.9%	15.4%
Restaurants & hotels	12.6%	9.3%
Food & drink	10.8%	15.3%
Miscellaneous	9.7%	8.7%
Household goods	6.4%	7.1%
Clothing & footwear	5.6%	6.7%
Alcohol & tobacco	4.0%	3.8%
Telephones & post	2.5%	3.3%
Health	2.2%	4.3%
Education	1.9%	1.1%

as it is designed to reflect the average family's purchases in an average month.

Sometimes when economists look at the rate of CPI inflation they strip some components out, creating a measure which is referred to as 'core' or 'underlying' inflation. Food, alcohol, tobacco & petrol are typically removed either because they often move up and down sharply, or because they are influenced by the government. Food prices, for example, can be highly dependent on the (sometimes fickle) weather. Petrol prices can move around sharply with the variable cost of oil, while both petrol and tobacco prices are affected by how much duty/tax the government chooses to levy. By removing these items we can often get a better idea of the underlying inflation picture in an economy.

The graph below compares overall (or 'headline') CPI inflation to core, or underlying, inflation for the UK. The surge in oil and petrol prices in 2008 and 2009 can be seen clearly as headline inflation rises sharply but core inflation does not.

Headline and core inflation in the UK

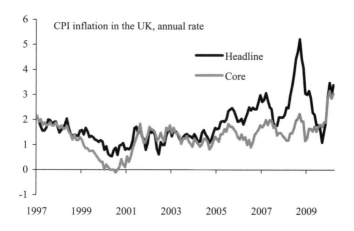

HOW PRICES ARE DETERMINED

Given that inflation is the rate of change in general prices, to explain inflation we need to understand how prices are determined. A bit of very basic economic theory will help here.

The most important lesson of economics is that the price of something depends on the demand for it compared with how much can be supplied. This applies not just to the price of the goods & services we buy but also to the cost of borrowing money – the interest rate – and the wages people receive in return for working.

For the time being, however, let's focus on the general price of goods & services. The amount of goods & services in the economy that households would like to buy (something we call 'aggregate demand') will depend on a whole host of things, including peoples' incomes, the cost of borrowing, how confident we are about the future, and – perhaps most importantly of all – the price at which those goods & services are being sold.

Imagine all of the influences on the amount of goods & services we want to buy stay the same – apart from prices. How then might our demand change when prices move up and down? It seems reasonable to think that we would want to buy more goods & services when they are cheaper, and less when they are more expensive. This inverse relationship between price and quantity demanded is shown by the downward sloping 'aggregate demand' line in the graph overleaf.

Now let's think about supply. How does the quantity of goods & services that retailers are willing to supply change with price? Again, let's assume all of the other factors influencing their decision, other than prices, stay the same. Retailers would probably be willing to offer more

How demand and supply interact to determine prices

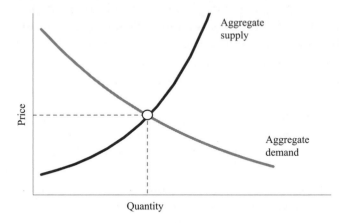

goods & services for sale when the price is higher, and less when it is lower. This relationship is opposite to that of demand, and is shown by the upward sloping line in the graph above (we've labelled this 'aggregate supply').

The point at which the demand and supply curves are the same – i.e. where the lines cross in the graph above – shows some kind of balance, or 'equilibrium'. Here, the price has been determined that will clear the market. At this price, the amount of goods & services that households demand will be exactly the same as that which firms are willing to supply.

This simple theory helps explain the two main causes of inflation that economists distinguish between: demand-pull and cost-push inflation. Let's take a look at these now.

WHO YOU NEED TO KNOW
Alfred Marshall

The charts you see in this chapter illustrating how the interaction of demand and supply leads to prices being formed were first envisaged by Alfred Marshall in his seminal 1890 book, *Principles of Economics*. This analysis has stood the test of time – it remains the way that basic economics is taught in schools and universities today.

He described the lines in these figures as the *laws of supply and demand* – that firms are willing to supply more while people will demand less as the price of goods & services rise, and vice versa. Associated with these laws was something he called 'elasticity': *how much* demand and supply changes in response to a change in price. As an example, households' demand for food tends to be *inelastic* – in other words, people do not usually reduce the amount of food they eat that much when prices go up. After all, we still need to eat, whatever the price. In contrast, demand for items that might be considered luxuries – such as a new handbag, for example – may fall sharply when prices go up (demand is said to be *elastic*).

Marshall also had something to say about currencies. He argued that the exchange rate between two countries should reflect the relative prices of goods & services in those countries. In other words if, say, the price of an iPod was £150 in the UK but $300 in the US, then a floating exchange rate should move towards $2 per £1.

What Alfred Marshall will be remembered for more than anything else, however, was his ability to visualise economics in relatively simple – but revolutionary at the time – charts. That economics has become a formal academic and scientific discipline is the result of his work.

CAUSES OF INFLATION: DEMAND-PULL VERSUS COST-PUSH

So, we now know how the general level of prices is determined in an economy. But what causes these 'equilibrium' prices to rise? In other words, what causes inflation?

Economists like to distinguish between two types of inflation, depending on what triggers the rise in prices: 'demand-pull' and 'cost-push'. Demand-pull, as its name suggests, is inflation that results from higher demand for goods & services. Cost-push inflation, on the other hand, occurs when firms face a rise in costs which are then passed on to their customers in the form of higher prices. Let's have a look at these two types of inflation in more detail.

1. Demand-Pull

Perhaps the best way to describe this type of inflation is a quote from Milton Friedman, the monetary economist, who said that inflation is caused by, 'too much money chasing too few goods'.

To explain, imagine that everyone in the country either had more money – perhaps due to a rise in their take-home pay – or simply wanted to spend a larger portion of their existing income (i.e. by saving less). This might happen for a number of reasons: higher take home pay may be due to a tax cut (which raises people's available income), while spending more may be the result of increased confidence about the future (encouraging people to save less, perhaps because they are less fearful about becoming unemployed).

At any given price, people now want to buy more goods & services than they did before, because of their improved circumstances. In other words, the whole demand curve from the graph on page 46 will move to the right – as is shown in the graph below.

Now, if firms know there's more demand for their product, they will reasonably want to raise their price.

Demand-pull inflation

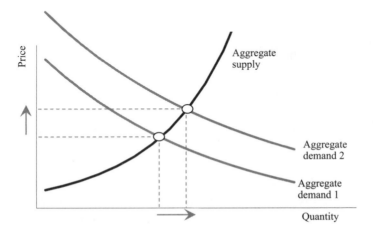

If they didn't increase prices, then households would want to buy too much relative to what firms would be willing to supply. In the end, households buy more from firms at higher prices, as the previous graph shows. This new equilibrium is the only point at which both firms and households are simultaneously happy about the amount (and price) of what they are selling/buying.

Demand-pull inflation is the sort of inflation we get when we are in the boom phase of the business cycle, and economic output is running above its trend or potential level. Remember that we looked at this in the first chapter – it's when we have a positive output gap (point Y in the graph on page 21). It should be clear now why we described this difference between output and its trend level as being an *inflationary* or *deflationary* gap – because the strength or weakness of the economy can cause prices to rise or fall.

As demand for goods & services becomes higher and higher, it might become increasingly difficult for firms to expand capacity to meet that demand. This is why the supply line in the graph above becomes steeper at the top – at this point, a rise in demand would result more in price rises than in rising quantities traded.

The way that the authorities usually address the problem of rising inflation caused by too much demand is to raise interest rates, which encourages saving and discourages borrowing. This in turn reduces the desire of households to spend money and firms to invest, thus limiting peoples' demand for goods & services. We will look in more detail later in the book at how central banks, such as the Bank of England in the UK, the Federal Reserve in the US and the European Central Bank in Europe, use interest rates to control inflation.

2. Cost-Push

So, to recap, demand-pull inflation happens when the desire of households to buy goods & services puts too much pressure on the ability of firms to supply it. But what about cost-push inflation?

Cost-push inflation happens when it becomes more expensive for firms to supply their goods & services. Let's have a think about the ways in which this might occur by going back to our handbag producer from the first chapter. An important raw material that our producer needs to make handbags is leather. Imagine now that the price of leather on world commodity markets rises.

Another way that producers' costs might rise is through a fall in the value of the currency. In that case, even if the price of leather in, say, US dollars on global commodity markets remains the same, because the domestic currency cannot buy as many dollars it will cost more for our handbag producer to import.

Whatever the reason, in economics terminology the producer's input prices have risen (remember this from the diagram on page 41). In order to compensate for this and maintain its profit margins, the producer then raises the price at which it sells the final product (the handbag) to retailers – the output price. And in turn, the retailer then attempts to pass this price rise on to the final consumer (by raising consumer prices).

Two of the most significant periods of cost-push inflation occurred in the 1970s, and were caused by the disruption to global oil supplies. In 1973/74 and 1978/79 oil prices soared, raising producers' costs and then inflation significantly – especially in those economies that were heavily dependent on oil. In the UK, for example, inflation reached a peak of 24% in 1975 and, after a brief period of respite, rose back up to 18% in 1980.

How can we show cost-push inflation on our demand/ supply figure? This time it is the supply (rather than the demand) curve that moves. Because of the rise in their costs, firms will now only be willing to supply goods or services at a higher price – if they didn't raise their prices then profits would go down. This means that supply curve has moved to the left, as shown in the following graph.

In this case, the end result is that prices go up (i.e. we get inflation) but activity falls – people want to buy

Cost-push inflation

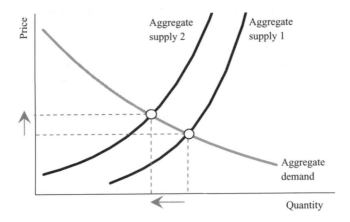

less because prices have gone up. In the extreme what can happen is that higher costs – which get passed on through the economy from producers to retailers and then consumers – cause something called 'stagflation'. This is a combination of *stag*nation (or even worse a fall) in activity but at the same time high in*flation*. The 1970s oil price rises were examples of this – the sharp rise in inflation proved to be a significant brake on economic activity.

In reality, it can be difficult to distinguish between demand-pull and cost-push inflation, as rising demand can cause higher commodity prices and wages (both of which are costs to firms). The two types of inflation can (and often do), therefore, happen simultaneously.

WHO YOU NEED TO KNOW
Milton Friedman

Milton Friedman was a free-market 'monetarist' economist, arguing (against Keynes) that government intervention in the economy was inappropriate. In the 1950s and 1960s when he undertook his most important work, for which he later won a Nobel Prize in Economics, this was an opposite conclusion to the interventionist approach of governments worldwide.

His first key work looked at consumer spending. While Keynes argued that household spending should depend on *current* earnings, Friedman believed it was one's expected lifetime (or 'permanent') earnings that would be more important. This gave him a basis to argue against government intervention – tax cuts, for example, would be seen by people as being temporary so they wouldn't spend so much of their extra disposable income (they would save it instead, which would do little to support economic activity).

In the early 1960s Friedman turned his attention to the money supply. He was a firm believer in the 'Quantity Theory of Money', which says that money can have a strong influence on prices. The early years of Thatcherism in the UK were based on Friedman's work – the Bank of England was given the task of targeting the money supply as that was seen as the key to controlling inflation. In the event, not only did it prove difficult to achieve the monetary targets set by the government, but the policy fell foul of Friedman's warning that the effect of money on inflation would be subject to 'long and variable lags'.

Towards the end of the 1960s Friedman came up with a theory for which he is perhaps best known. He argued there exists in all economies a natural – or equilibrium – rate of unemployment. If a government attempted to intervene to reduce the rate below this level then it would simply end up resulting in inflation and no improvement in either unemployment or economic activity. The 1970s period of 'stagflation' – a weak economy combined with high inflation – proved him right.

THE IMPORTANCE OF INFLATION

So far we have described what inflation is and looked at two ways it can be generated – by rising demand or costs. But why do economists care so much about inflation? The answer is that high and unpredictable inflation can be bad for an economy.

WHO SAID IT

"Inflation is as violent as a mugger, as frightening as an armed robber and as deadly as a hit man."
– **Ronald Reagan**

The most important problems and side-effects associated with inflation are as follows:

▶ *It's bad for savers.* Imagine you've locked your money away in a bank for five years at a fixed rate of 3% per year. As long as prices grow at a slower rate then you'd be able to buy more goods & services with your money when you come to take it out. But what if there was an unexpected surge in inflation, with prices rising by more than the interest you make on your money? By the end of your investment your money would buy you less than when you started. It's not just savers who lose out, but all people who receive a fixed income. Pensioners, for example, may be out of pocket if their pensions do not rise at least as quickly as the rate of inflation. Inflation thus causes a loss of purchasing power and a reduction in living standards for some people, and may discourage saving.

▶ *It's good for borrowers.* While it's bad for savers, a bout of inflation can be good for borrowers. Higher than expected inflation means that a bank lending money to a borrower may have set the interest rate it charges on the loan too low to account for the rise in the cost of living. The borrower then benefits by paying less interest than the bank would have demanded had it known that inflation was going to be high. Note that it is only *unexpected* inflation which causes these problems, as if it were expected it would have been built into higher interest rates in the first place.

▶ *It can cause higher interest rates.* Particularly when inflation is caused by higher spending, the authorities may raise interest rates to cool demand in the economy. But that raises the risk of causing too sharp a downturn in the economy, or even a recession.

▶ *It can influence when you buy.* If prices are falling you may be tempted to wait before buying that flat screen television you've had your eye on. But if prices are rising quickly, then you may want to bring forward your purchases before prices get too high.

▶ *It's bad for investment.* Firms like certainty when planning their business ventures. If they are unsure about what the inflation rate is going to be then they may demand a higher return on their investment to compensate for the possibility that their costs rise more sharply. By raising the hurdle, fewer investments may be made. Another way that inflation is bad for investment is that, as we saw above, it discourages savings in the economy. And if banks receive fewer funds from savers then they can't lend as much out to businesses for investment. Instead, rather than saving in a bank, high inflation may encourage people to put their money assets like houses or gold, which are less productive than the money being lent out for investment.

▶ *It causes 'shoe leather' costs.* When inflation is high it encourages people to search out the best prices as there may be significant differences across retailers. Shoe leather costs refer to the increased cost of search in terms of one's time and effort (in literal terms it wears out the soles of your shoes!).

▶ *It increases 'menu costs'.* When inflation is high it means firms need to change the prices of their goods & services more often – which can be costly. Think of a restaurant that has to continually reprint its menus because the price is changing so quickly. Technology has helped reduce these costs (online retailers, for example, can change their prices at the touch of a button) but High Street retailers will incur the cost of having to change their prices on the shelves more regularly when inflation is higher.

▶ *It can generate a wage-price spiral.* A problem with rising prices is that they encourage workers to bargain for higher pay to compensate. But, as we learned when we looked at both demand-pull and cost-push inflation, if wages are higher that may lead to higher prices. In turn, workers then ask for higher wages and the upward spiral continues. Moreover, if wages rise by more than tax thresholds do, then workers will eventually move into higher tax brackets because of this spiral – something that economists call 'fiscal drag'.

▶ *It's bad for competitiveness.* If price rises are not followed by a fall in the currency, then the price of that country's goods & services may begin to look uncompetitive to overseas importers who will demand fewer goods & services from that country.

As a result of these costs, over the past 20 years central banks have been focusing their attention on targeting inflation – trying to keep it stable and at a low pre-announced level in order to provide an environment that is conducive to strong economic growth.

So, ideally, we would like inflation to be low, stable and predictable. But history has shown this isn't always easy to achieve. Let's now turn our attention to two extremes – first, when prices actually fall rather than rise (deflation) and second, at the opposite end of the spectrum, when prices rise at an excessively fast rate (hyperinflation).

Extreme 1: Deflation

Let's start with deflation. Deflation is precisely the opposite of inflation – it is when we see a sustained decline in the general level of prices or, in other words, when the rate of inflation falls below zero. It is important to distinguish this from a period of *dis-inflation*, which is when the rate of inflation (as opposed to the level of prices) is falling.

Just as inflation can be caused by a rise in demand for goods & services, deflation is typically caused by weaker demand. In the graph on page 50 weaker demand can be shown by moving the demand to the left – imagine starting with Aggregate Demand 2 and moving to

Aggregate Demand 1. In this case, weaker demand causes both prices and the amount of goods & services demanded to fall. This is demand-pull inflation in reverse.

It is not only weaker demand that can cause deflation. Imagine if all suppliers were able to now produce at lower cost – perhaps, for example, because of some technological innovation. They would then be able to supply those goods & services to the retailer at a lower price, who in turn could pass on the savings to households. This is cost-push inflation in reverse. In the graph on page 54 we can show this by starting from Aggregate Supply 2 and moving to Aggregate Supply 1. This is a much better type of deflation than that caused by a shortage of demand, because it tends to increase activity in the economy and does not necessarily cause the problems that deflation led by lower demand does.

So, what *is* so bad about demand-led deflation? Well, once deflation has started it can be exceptionally difficult for a country to get out of. Let's say an initial fall in peoples' demand for goods & services causes a fall in prices. People may then expect prices to continue falling in the future – in which case they would delay making their purchases. After all, in a year's time the price may be lower, so they would get more for their money. But by postponing their purchases they are causing a further drop in demand now, which leads to higher unemployment, lower incomes, and a further fall in prices – perpetuating the downward spiral. This deflation trap is shown in the following diagram. Deflation may also cause

The deflationary spiral

Initial fall in demand → Prices drop → Demand falls further as purchases are delayed → Prices drop because of lower demand

businesses to invest less and employ fewer people (just as they might in a high inflation environment) because lower prices mean lower profits, reducing the incentive to produce.

Deflation can be even worse when levels of debt in an economy are high. Just as high inflation can help borrowers of money, they lose out in periods of deflation. With deflation, prices and wages fall, making it more difficult for households to service their existing debts – the value of which doesn't fall, of course. In other words, deflation causes the real (or inflation-adjusted) amount of people's debt to rise.

This encourages people to pay off their debts – but to do so they must sell the assets against which the loans were made (houses, for example). But the selling of assets leads to a fall in their price, a weaker economy and thus a further fall in general prices – and so the cycle continues. This theory of 'debt-deflation' was originally proposed by the US economist Irving Fisher during the Great Depression of the early 1930s.

The two cases that come to mind when we think about deflation are Japan over the past 20 years, and the US during the 1930s Great Depression. In Japan, deflation began in the early 1990s after the collapse of the housing and stock market bubbles that had built up during the previous decade. Loans that had been made by banks in the good times began to turn sour, causing a financial crisis when borrowers failed to repay. Banks were unwilling (or unable) to lend money, causing the economy to weaken and prices to fall, generating an ongoing deflationary spiral.

In the early 1930s, during a period of sharply lower economic activity, the US experienced a period during which prices were falling by up to 10% per year. As in Japan, the Great Depression was preceded by sharp rises in share prices during the 1920s, the collapse of which led to a drying up of credit availability. The situation was made worse by the Federal Reserve – America's central bank – initially failing to stop the money supply from shrinking. President Roosevelt's 'New Deal' policies announced in 1933 finally helped the US economy out of recession and deflation.

One of the reasons that central banks try to keep inflation at a positive, but low, rate is that if they were to aim for zero there would be too great a risk of prices falling and a deflationary cycle becoming entrenched.

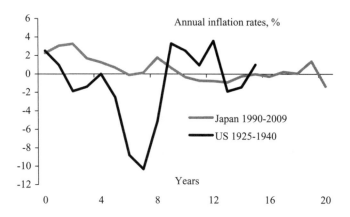

Deflation in Japan (1990s/2000s) and the US (1930s)

Extreme 2: Hyperinflation

The polar opposite of deflation is hyperinflation. There is no agreed definition of what level of inflation constitutes hyperinflation but some have classified it as being when inflation approaches 50% *per month* (you know that inflation is out of control when you begin to talk about it in monthly rather than annual rates!). Generally speaking, however, it is when inflation is so high that it becomes completely uncontrollable and leads to an exceptionally quick decline in the value of money.

In the past, the most serious hyperinflations have been caused when central banks have printed too much money in order to fund government borrowing – often in the aftermath of war. Hyperinflation can be seen as a particularly extreme version of the demand-pull inflation we looked at above. In Germany, for example, between 1922 and 1923 inflation ran at an average rate of over 300% per month (a doubling in prices every three weeks), while in Hungary after the Second World War inflation ran at a staggering average rate of 20000% per month between 1945 and 1946 (a doubling in prices every five days – and, at its peak, every half day). More recent examples include Yugoslavia in 1994 and Zimbabwe at the end of the last decade.

When prices are rising so quickly the whole monetary system breaks down. In past instances of hyperinflation workers have had to be paid daily, paid with huge volumes of bank notes – so large, in fact, that rather than carrying their day's pay home in their wallet they had to resort to wheelbarrows! Confidence in money evaporates, and people want to rid themselves of it as quickly as possible before its value goes down – in turn leading to hoarding of goods.

Remedies for hyperinflation vary from using a foreign currency as the means of exchange to completely over-hauling the country's existing currency. But, to have any chance of success, these policies would have to co-exist with the government slashing the amount it borrows, and the central bank maintaining far tighter control over the money supply.

Fortunately governments and central banking globally have learned the lessons of excessive money printing. While the authorities do still create additional money during economic downturns (so called 'quantitative easing', which we will look at in more depth in the chapter on central banks), these policies are generally designed to support demand and prevent inflation from falling too much, rather than being used irresponsibly as a tool to fund government borrowing.

A Yugoslavian 500 billion dinar note

WHO SAID IT

"By a continuing process of inflation, government can confiscate, secretly and unobserved, an important part of the wealth of their citizens."
– John Maynard Keynes

EXPECTATIONS

Inflation expectations can play an important role in economic decision making. To see why, consider some of the costs of inflation we looked at earlier. The cost to savers of inflation, for example, is higher when the fixed interest rate they receive does not take into account an unexpected rise in inflation in the future. Firms planning to invest may not do so if they can't make a reasonable guess about where inflation will be going forward. People may delay or accelerate their purchases of goods & services depending on what they think is going to happen to prices. And workers may bid for higher wages if they think prices are going to rise more quickly, in turn risking a wage-price spiral (whereby higher inflation expectations become a self-fulfilling prophecy).

So, as you can see, inflation expectations can have an important effect not only on economic activity but also on actual future inflation. A central bank that can keep inflation expectations under wraps, or 'anchored' as it is termed, will have a much better chance at keeping actual inflation low too. The way that central banks can achieve this is to earn people's trust – to prove that they actually mean it when they say they will set interest rates to ensure that inflation remains low and stable. In economists' language, the central bank must be 'credible'.

How do people form their expectations of future inflation? There are two main theories: 'adaptive' and 'rational' expectations. Adaptive expectations means that people base their view of *future* inflation on where inflation was in *the past* (an example of this might be the view that if inflation is high now, then it will remain so in the future). Rational expectations, on the other hand, are when individuals think about all the factors that might influence inflation in the future and make their best judgment based on that. As with many things in economics, what people actually do is probably some combination of the two.

If we can anticipate future inflation with some certainty, then we can account for it in what we decide to do today – which ensures we make more informed decisions and reduces the costs we might incur from inflation. A believable central bank can go a long way to making this happen.

A HISTORY OF INFLATION

We are fortunate to have inflation figures going back over a very long time – to the eleventh century in the UK and the fifteenth century in the US, for example. While inflation is now based on a cross section of prices in a typical person's shopping basket, hundreds of years ago the collection of statistical data was not as advanced – we have to judge the rate of inflation back then by looking at grain prices.

Inflation in the UK and US and a number of other developed economies (Germany in the 1920s being a notable exception) was dormant before the 1970s, at

Inflation is a relatively recent phenomenon for some countries

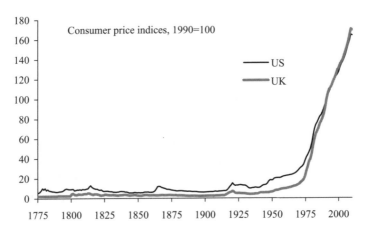

Consumer price indices, 1990=100

——— US

——— UK

which point stagflation reared its ugly head (as the previous graph shows). Governments have learned some of the lessons from this episode, and since the early 1990s inflation has generally been kept under much tighter control.

There are a number of reasons that inflation has performed better over recent years, including:

- ▶ the move towards targeting inflation – New Zealand's central bank started the trend in 1990 – helping reduce inflation expectations;
- ▶ the increase in competition that globalisation has brought – remember, the greater the supply of anything (in this case goods & services and jobs from abroad) the lower its price will be
- ▶ the reduction in costs due to the technological revolution and the associated boost to productivity (in particular the arrival of the internet in the early 1990s); and
- ▶ in the UK the strength of the exchange rate from the middle of the 1990s to around the time the credit crunch began, cutting the cost of imports.

Indeed, because of these factors the economy was able to perform better than in previous decades without causing inflation – a situation which has been described as the 'Great Moderation' or, in the words of Bank of England governor Mervyn King, the 'NICE' (Non-Inflationary Consistently Expansionary!) decade. Some

The 'Great Moderation' or NICE decade in the UK

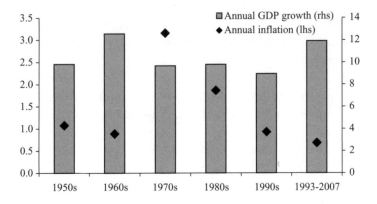

of these beneficial changes may prove more lasting than others, but it seems unlikely that we will see quite as good a trade-off between strong economic growth and low inflation over the coming decades as we have in the past.

WHAT YOU NEED TO READ

▶ The Bank of England has an excellent web page which explains the importance of inflation in the context of setting interest rates: *www.bankofengland.co.uk/education/targett-wopointzero/inflation*. In particular, a pamphlet that explains the importance of keeping inflation low and stable is highly recommended reading: *www.bankofengland.co.uk/publications/other/monetary/lowinflation.pdf*.

▶ An entertaining eight-minute cartoon explaining demand-pull and cost-push inflation, the costs of inflation, how central banks attempt to control inflation, and deflation – featuring the '*Inflation Monster*'! – can be found on the European Central Bank's website: *www.ecb.int/ecb/educational*.

▶ To read more about the thoughts of the economists mentioned in this chapter (such as John Maynard Keynes, Milton Friedman and Alfred Marshall) and others see Steven Pressman, *Fifty Major Economists*. Routledge, 2006 (2nd edition).

▶ To understand some of the reasons behind the fall in inflation relative to the 1970s and 1980s see Roger Bootle, *The Death of Inflation*. Nicholas Brealey, 1997 (2nd edition).

IF YOU ONLY REMEMBER ONE THING

The price of anything is determined by demand and supply, and changes in either can cause inflation. Low and stable inflation is desirable, and we should be fearful of the extremes: deflation on the one hand, hyperinflation on the other.

WHAT IT'S ALL ABOUT

- ▶ How the labour market works and the measurement of jobs/unemployment
- ▶ How employment and wages are determined
- ▶ Different types of unemployment and why they exist
- ▶ How unemployment moves with economic activity
- ▶ The link between unemployment and inflation
- ▶ Recent changes to the structure of the labour market

INTRODUCTION

Along with economic growth and inflation, the number of people employed or unemployed in the economy are among the most important of economic indicators. In the UK you'll often hear political parties point-scoring, arguing over how joblessness changed under current or previous governments. How the number of people in work in America changes from one month to the next is probably the single most important piece of economic news influencing financial markets around the world.

The reason employment – and for that matter unemployment – is so important is that it has a direct bearing on peoples' lives and the wellbeing of society as a whole. The number of people with jobs governs the total amount of wages that people take home. Remember from the circular flow of income in Chapter 1 that households use their incomes to spend on goods & services. When unemployment rises incomes fall, spending is lower, and firms may be forced to lay off even more staff as demand for their output declines. It's not difficult to see how a downward spiral in economic activity and employment can be created.

We begin by looking at a few basic definitions and explaining how the jobs – or labour – market fits together. In most countries the total population of 'working age' is made up of anyone who is over 16 but younger than the retirement age. The vast majority of these people will be in employment – whether they be full-time, part-time, temporary or self-employed workers. But some will be out of work and looking for a job – this is the level of unemployment. Together, the employed and unemployed are what we term 'active' in the jobs market because they are either working or looking for work. You may also hear the number of active people being referred to as the 'labour force' or the level of 'participation'.

But some people of working age are neither employed *nor* looking for a job. For one reason or another they are not interested in – or able to – work. We refer to these people as 'inactive'. There are a number of reasons that someone may be inactive: they are students, they have opted to look after the home rather than work, they are sick, they have entered early retirement, or they are discouraged – they are not looking for work because they believe there are no jobs available.

The following chart shows how all of this fits together. But how do we put numbers on each of these types of people?

MEASURING JOBS AND JOBLESSNESS

We can look at employment and unemployment in terms of both absolute numbers as well as rates. For example, following the recession of 2008–09, the level of employment in the UK had fallen to just under 27.5 million people, which was around 72% of the working age

How the jobs market fits together

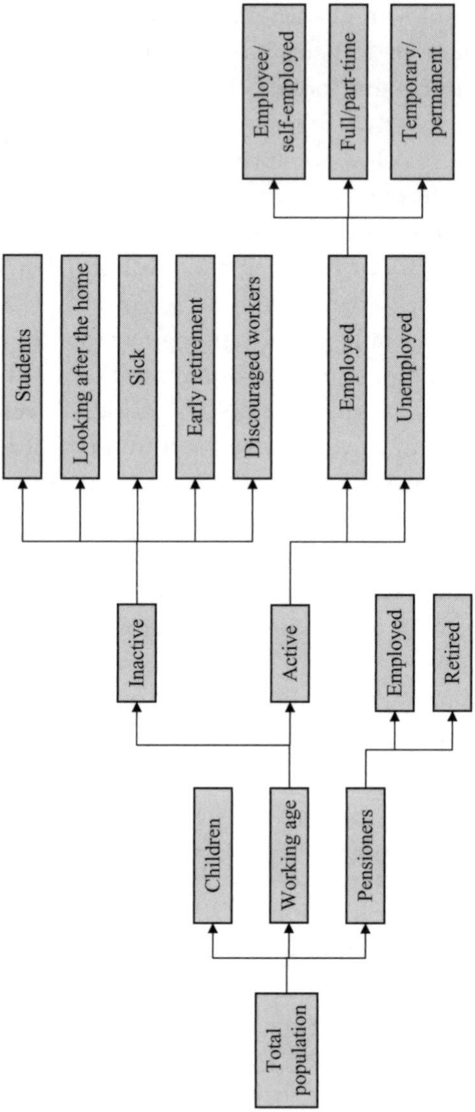

WHO YOU NEED TO KNOW
Thomas Malthus

Thomas Malthus is probably best known for his views on population, but also wrote on unemployment, trade and state-provided welfare. His *Essay on the Principle of Population* (1798) was written as an argument against those who believed that the government should provide help to the working classes.

He argued that the population would, if left unchecked, mushroom over time, but that food production could only grow at a steady pace. The reason food could not grow as quickly was that there was a limited amount of land, and that the most productive land was already under cultivation. Thus increasing the amount of food would require the use of land that yielded less.

While he suggested the use of birth control to limit the rise in the population, he also said that this would probably not be enough to prevent famine – a somewhat more drastic way of controlling the population. Malthus said that by redistributing wealth to the poor the government could be making matters worse, encouraging an increase in the birth rate and leading to higher food prices through greater demand. It's hardly surprising that Malthus' work earned the subject of economics the title of the 'Dismal Science' (courtesy of nineteenth century historian Thomas Carlyle).

His views on recessions were that they were caused by insufficient demand following a boom. During the boom phase, capitalists would have experienced rapidly rising profits which could not be invested quickly enough back into the economy – and they may not have wanted to because of labour shortages and resultant higher wages. Malthus' solution to this problem was straightforward – redistribute income away from the capitalists and towards land owners who were considered more likely to spend it.

population. Likewise, the number of people who were unemployed had risen to 2.4 million, or 8% of the working age population.

WHO SAID IT

"Economics is extremely useful as a form of employment for economists."
– John Kenneth Galbraith

In most countries, these figures are reported on a monthly basis by national statistics offices. Usually they are measured by a large survey of households which asks about their current status. The International Labour Organisation (ILO) – which is an agency of the United Nations – lays down guidelines about who exactly is classified as employed or unemployed, making it easier for us to compare the figures across countries. For example, under these definitions someone is classified as unemployed if they have been looking for work in the past four weeks and are available to start in the next two.

To complicate matters, however, there is another way that countries can estimate employment – by a survey of *firms* rather than *households*. Firm surveys tell us about the number of *jobs* rather than the number of *people in jobs*. The two may differ to the extent that some people have more than one job. The trends in both measures tend to be similar to one another, as the graph below shows, although they can vary from month to month.

While the household survey is the main indicator of employment in the UK, the focus in the US is on the firm (or 'establishment') survey. This measure of employment is also known as 'non-farm payrolls' – it tells us the number of jobs (outside of agriculture) and how they change on a monthly basis. This is probably the most important monthly economic statistic you'll ever come

Firm and household surveys of US employment

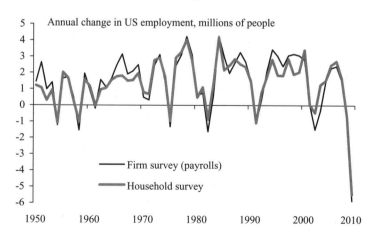

across, because it is crucial in influencing interest rate decisions made by the world's largest central bank – the US Federal Reserve. The reason for this is that the US is such as consumer-centric economy: employment – and thus household income too – is a key determinant of consumer demand and therefore overall economic activity.

Not only is there more than one way of reporting *employment*, but the same is true of *unemployment*. Rather than our survey of households, we can instead add up the number of people who are actually claiming unemployment benefits from the state. This usually reports a lower total for unemployment than the household survey, because not all people who say they are unemployed in that survey collect their benefits. In the UK, for example, the so called 'claimant count' measure of unemployment stood at about 4.5% in the middle of 2010, compared to the 8% on the household survey measure.

The problem with looking at the number of people claiming unemployment benefits as a measure of the jobless total is that it can be subject to government manipulation. If, for example, a government were to reduce the number of weeks they allowed unemployed people to claim benefits (in order to incentivise employment) that might make the numbers look artificially lower than was really the case. During Margaret Thatcher's tenure as Prime Minister in the 1980s is was reported that the UK government changed the definition of unemployment around 30 times – with most of these changes leading to a lower level of unemployment. Still, the number of claimants has two distinct advantages as a measure of unemployment: first, it is hard data rather than being based on a survey, and second it tends to be reported earlier than the surveys.

THE JOBS MARKET AND WAGES

What influences the number of people in work and the amount of pay they receive? Remember from Chapter 2 that the prices of goods & services are influenced by how much people want to buy in relation to their availability. The greater is demand relative to supply, the higher will be the price. The same is true in the jobs market, but this time instead of goods & services we are looking at the demand and supply of hours worked, with the 'price' being peoples' hourly wage rate.

As suppliers of labour, individuals would probably be willing to work longer hours if their wage is increased. But firms will probably demand more workers the cheaper they are to hire. We show this as the two bold lines in the following graph. Now imagine what happens if the prices of goods & services in the shops rise. Both of the lines in the figure would move upwards because individuals would want higher wages to compensate them, and firms would be willing to offer higher wages because they can sell the output that workers make for a higher price.

How wages and employment interact

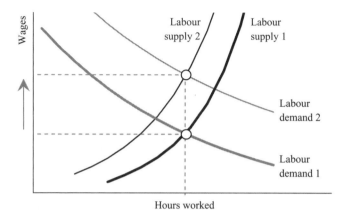

So, higher prices mean higher wages, but – as the graph above shows – not necessarily any change in how much people work. The reason that people are left in exactly the same situation as they started is as follows: they receive a higher hourly wage, but they need that to buy the same amount of goods as they did before, when both prices and wage rates were lower. In *real* terms, nothing has changed.

What we've looked at above is called the Classical Theory of wages and employment. Economists like boiling real world issues such as jobs and pay down to simplistic explanations like this, but in reality things can be more complicated. When deciding whether to take a job or how many hours to work, a prospective employee will be interested in more than just wages. For example, he or she must take into consideration the amount that they could receive from the government by not working and instead claiming state benefits. The higher the level of unemployment benefits compared to wages (something which economists call the 'replacement ratio') the more likely it will be that an individual opts not to work.

TYPES OF UNEMPLOYMENT

In any economy at any point in time there are always people without jobs who want them. In trying to understand why unemployment exists, we can classify it into various different types – depending on the cause. There are five major types of unemployment:

Structural. The level of unemployment that is associated with the normal operation of the economy is called structural unemployment. This usually exists because of the long-term decline of particular industries in a country and the inability of the people previously employed in those industries to retrain for other jobs. Think of the manufacturing firms in the UK (car assembly, shipyards, steel workers for example) that have succumbed to the intense competition of low cost production in emerging markets like China. It may be difficult to retrain these redundant workers for office-based employment.

This type of unemployment may be the result of technological progress which reduces the need for workers as opposed to machines. Because of its nature – requiring workers to retrain for different jobs – structural unemployment tends to be long-term, with the people it affects often being out of work for a year or longer).

Cyclical. Cyclical unemployment, as the name suggests, results from a slowdown in the economy. It is also sometimes called 'demand-deficient' unemployment because, during a recession or slowdown, demand falls prompting firms to produce fewer goods & services and thereby lay off some of their staff. Typically, when the economy is growing at a rate below its trend we would expect to see cyclical unemployment rise, and when the economy is growing above its trend cyclical unemployment should fall.

Classical. Too much interference in the labour market can be the cause of higher unemployment. We saw above that if left to their own devices employment and wages will be determined by how many man hours firms want and how many workers are willing to supply. But what happens if unions try to keep wages too high? Or if the government were to set a minimum wage that was too high? Well, we can safely assume that more individuals would want to work because they are receiving a greater reward, but firms wouldn't want to hire as many people because of the additional expense. In other words, unemployment rises.

The following chart shows for various countries the average rates of unemployment over the past 15–20 years.

Average unemployment rates across countries

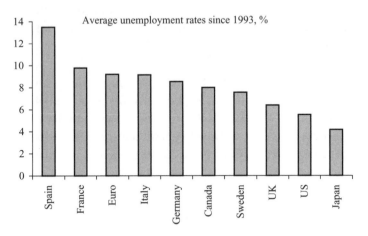

Average unemployment rates since 1993, %

In the euro area unemployment has tended to be higher than in other countries such as the UK, US and Japan. One of the reasons for this may be that the labour markets of these countries are so tightly controlled and rigid – something that has been called 'euro-sclerosis'. For example, there are high costs associated with laying off workers, unions are more powerful and unemployment benefits tend to be higher. In other words, workers are being priced out of the market. Some European economies are moving towards the freeing up of their labour markets, but it will be a slow process to reduce this classical unemployment.

Frictional. If a person loses their job it may take some time to search for a new one – even if the economic cycle is strong and jobs are plentiful. This is called frictional unemployment, and exists because of what economists call 'imperfect information' (job vacancies may exist, but it takes time before the firm and the prospective employee discover each other) and the geographical immobility of some workers (the firm and employee are physically not in the same place). It has been suggested that lowering unemployment benefit payments may encourage people to search for jobs quicker and reduce frictional unemployment.

Seasonal. Changes in employment and unemployment can be caused by seasonal influences. More people tend to be hired in the run up to Christmas, for example, than during the rest of the year. Think of the increase in temporary sales staff to cope with the increase in festive purchases in the shops. Unemployment will tend to be rise back in the New Year, however, as spending drops off again. In reality unemployment statistics are usually adjusted to smooth out such seasonal influences in a similar way to the GDP figures, as we saw in Chapter 1.

Most of these measures of unemployment are what we'd call 'involuntary' – in other words it is not by choice that people are out of work. In the case of cyclical and seasonal unemployment it is because of a fall in demand in the economy; frictional is due to the delay in finding a new job; and structural is because of the long-term decline of a particular industry. All are out of the hands of workers.

It is a different matter when it comes to classical unemployment, however. In this case, by asking for too high a wage, workers are essentially pricing themselves out of the jobs market. Were they to lower their demands then prospective employers may be more interested in hiring them. As a result classical unemployment is often referred to – possibly a little unfairly – as being 'voluntary'.

OKUN'S LAW

Let's take a closer look now at cyclical unemployment. We learned above that with cyclical unemployment, the number of people without a job rises when the economy performs poorly, and falls when it performs well. This is what is known as 'Okun's Law' after the economist Arthur Okun who, back in the early 1960s, wrote about the relationship between economic growth and the unemployment rate in the United States. Okun originally pointed out that a 3% rise in economic activity would be associated with a 1% drop in the unemployment rate, and vice versa.

If only it were this simple! In practice, the way unemployment moves when the economy strengthens or weakens can vary quite substantially. Take a look at the following chart, for example. This shows for a number of countries during the most recent recession the rise in the unemployment rate plotted on the horizontal axis against the fall in GDP on the vertical axis.

Unemployment and activity across countries

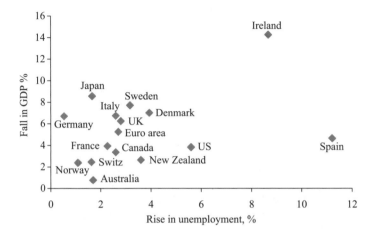

As you can see, there are big cross-country differences in the way that unemployment responds to economic activity. Countries such as the US and Spain suffered large rises in their unemployment rates relative to the economic contraction during the last recession. On the other hand, Germany and Japan experienced smaller increases in their unemployment rates compared to how sharply economic activity fell. These differences may be due to a number of factors, including so called labour rigidities (by supporting wages and hours worked trade unions may be forcing firms to reduce the size of their workforce to save money during a recession) and the fact that certain sectors are more labour intensive than others (think of the size of Spain's construction sector, for example, which was hit by a weaker housing market).

So, we've established that the way economic growth and joblessness interact can vary quite substantially across countries. But how unemployment – or, on the other side of the coin, employment – changes with economic growth can vary markedly over time in the *same country*. The chart overleaf shows how the number of people employed in the UK has changed as economic activity has swung up and down over the past 30 years.

WHO SAID IT

"It's a recession when your neighbour loses his job; it's a depression when you lose your own."
– **Harry S Truman**

In the recession that followed the credit crunch in 2008–09, employment in the UK did not fall anywhere near as sharply as past history suggests it might have. While GDP fell from peak to trough by more than in any other post-war recession, the fall in employment was less than it was in the recessions of the early 1990s, 1980s or 1970s.

Unemployment and activity over time in the UK

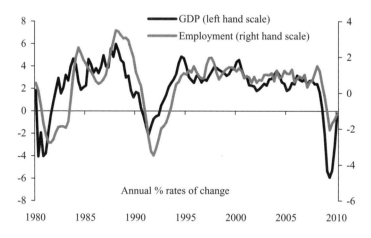

Why was this the case? It could have been that people were willing to work for lower wages or work part time, reducing firms' wage bills and thereby encouraging them to retain their staff through the recession. In addition the government continued hiring during the downturn, offsetting some of the recession-related fall in private sector jobs. And it might also have been that changes in economic policy (such as sharply lower interest rates) helped companies to weather the recession better.

TIME LAGS

One thing you might have noticed from the chart above is that economic activity seems to change before employment does – not by long, probably only three months. We say that employment changes 'lag' changes in economic activity. Why does this happen?

Think of a typical manufacturer, who hires workers to make a product which is then bought by households. What happens if people start buying less of the firm's product – perhaps because the government has raised income taxes meaning that they have less disposable income to spend? The producer is then left with unsold goods, and might opt to reduce its workforce if it does not expect demand to recover.

But the producer must be careful – what if the fall in demand were to prove temporary? When people start buying more of the firm's product again the firm would be short of labour and have to re-hire workers. So, producers tend not to get rid of workers immediately when demand for their product falls because it is expensive to fire and then re-hire staff. Think of the payouts to staff involved in terminating their contracts, and the subsequent cost of searching for new employees when demand picks up again.

So firms will want to be cautious in reducing their workforce when a downturn comes. Likewise, in an upturn it may take some time to hire the staff that it needs to meet the extra demand for its product. In other words, there are time lags between changes in activity and employment in the upswing too.

PRODUCTIVITY

It is useful to think about what these time lags mean for productivity. Productivity is just the amount of output that an *average worker* in the economy produces. It can alternatively be measured as the amount of output produced during an *average hour* of work.

As we have seen, in a recession output falls first then employment follows shortly after. This means that for a time the same workforce is making less, and productivity falls. But in an upswing, because firms can't increase their staff as quick as activity is rising (remember frictional unemployment – it takes time for employees and employers to find one another), they have to use their existing workforce more intensively – which means that productivity rises. In other words – productivity moves in tune with the economic cycle.

What we really care about, though, when it comes to productivity is the *underlying* rate of improvement over time – not just the swings that result from the economy moving between recession and boom. Long run productivity is influenced by how efficiently the economy combines the three factors of production – natural resources (such as land), workers, and machines (or capital) – to make goods & services. Let's have a think about how changes in these factors can improve productivity:

> ▶ *Natural resources.* There's not really very much we can do about the natural resources a country

WHO YOU NEED TO KNOW
Adam Smith

Born in Scotland, Adam Smith is considered to be the father of economics – even though in his day the subject as we now know it didn't really exist (he started his scholarly life essentially as a philosopher). He is widely cited for his capitalist views, in particular his desire to promote competition in order to raise economic wellbeing.

He is best known for his book *The Wealth of Nations*, published in 1776. In it, he argued that if we all act in our own self interest then that will also be the best outcome for society as a whole. This is reflected in the most famous of Smith's quotes: an individual is, "led by an invisible hand to promote an end which was no part of his intention" – that end being to maximise national wealth.

He talked of how technological progress and the 'division of labour' could improve productivity. He used the example of a factory that made pins, arguing that if each worker was responsible for just one task in the pin-making process, output would be much larger than if each worker were to make whole pins themselves. Have a look on the reverse side of the UK's current £20 note and you'll see a portrait of Smith and a depiction of this division of labour. The most obvious present day example of this is in the car industry, where each worker focuses their attention on assembling just one part of the vehicle.

There are a number of reasons Smith said this process would improve productivity: repetition improves speed, time is saved by not moving from task to task, and workers are encouraged to devise time-saving machinery to help them with their specific job.

On another issue, Smith supported the idea of free trade, as lower-priced imports could reduce the cost of making goods for export. That put him at odds with the conventional wisdom at the time (known as 'Mercantilism') which said that wealth would be improved by *restricting* imports. Despite his focus on free trade and competition, Smith did not denounce the role of government entirely – laws to limit large companies and the provision of policing/national defence were important for the government to provide. Still, to this day Smith remains the torch-bearer for laissez-faire (literally 'let it be' in French) free-market economics.

is – or isn't as the case may be – bestowed with. This is the factor of production that can be least influenced by human intervention.

▶ *Labour.* Workers can always be incentivised to work harder and become more productive – perhaps by offering them shares in the company they work for, or by setting up profit-sharing schemes.

▶ *Capital.* Investing in either a greater number of, or more efficient, machines can increase the amount a worker can produce. Workers are often concerned about being displaced by new technology, but don't forget that it takes a skilled workforce to create improved technology in the first place.

The importance of achieving higher productivity is that it allows us to become better off by lowering the costs of production. And ageing populations in many countries makes productivity growth a necessity, as there are an increasing number of retired people relying on a smaller percentage of those still in work. So it is not surprising that the holy grail of governments is to raise the long-run growth rate of productivity.

THE PHILLIPS CURVE AND THE 'NATURAL RATE' OF UNEMPLOYMENT

One particularly important issue in macroeconomics over the past 50 years has been the relationship between unemployment and inflation. Economic thinking has shifted dramatically on this relationship, and in a way which has a crucial impact on policymaking – both the setting of interest rates and government decisions on taxation and spending.

In the late 1950s, the economist A.W. Phillips published a study which looked at inflation and unemployment in the United States over the previous century. He discovered that there was a clear relationship between wages and jobs – when the rate of unemployment fell wages tended to rise more sharply, and vice versa. The same was found to be true if prices, rather than wages, were compared to unemployment. The inverse relationship between inflation and the rate of unemployment soon became known as the 'Phillips Curve'.

It led to governments around the world concluding that they could decide what trade-off they wanted between the two evils of inflation and unemployment. For example, if a government believed *unemployment* to be too high it could reduce it by running expansionary policies (tax cuts, higher spending, or lower interest rates) but only at the expense of higher inflation. If, instead, the government believed that *inflation* was too high, then it could raise taxes, cut spending or raise interest rates to reduce demand and therefore inflation – this time at the cost of higher unemployment. In other words, according to Phillips, there was no 'free-lunch' – inflation and unemployment would not fall (or for that matter rise) at the same time.

The Phillips Curve

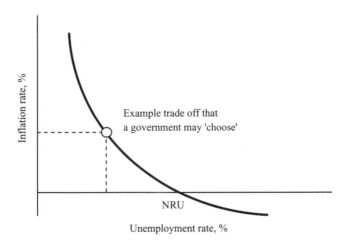

Unemployment rate, %

This all suggested there was a level of unemployment through which it was impossible to fall without causing prices to rise – a level that was referred to as the 'natural rate of unemployment', labelled as NRU in the chart above. At the natural rate we say we have 'full employment' – there are still people unemployed, but to raise employment/cut unemployment any further would cause other economic problems (inflation).

Another way of thinking about the natural rate of unemployment is by going back to the different types of unemployment we encountered earlier in the chapter. The natural rate is the level of unemployment that exists even if the economy is growing as it should be – in other words it's not due to a lack of demand. So, the natural rate can be thought of as the four other types of unemployment (structural, classical, frictional and seasonal) apart from cyclical.

As Okun's law suggested, governments can deal with cyclical unemployment by stimulating activity in the economy – so called 'demand management' policies. Alternatively, policies that are aimed instead at attempting to reduce the natural rate of unemployment by dealing with problems inherent in the structure of the labour market are called 'supply side' policies because they are dealing with the supply of labour. Curbing union power, providing better retraining and reforming unemployment benefits are the sort of supply side policies that can help reduce the Natural Rate of Unemployment.

WHY THE PHILLIPS CURVE STOPPED WORKING

The Phillips Curve seemed like a good description of how economies worked up until the end of the 1960s, but things changed dramatically in the following two decades. The combination of rising unemployment *and* inflation in a number of economies during the 1970s and 1980s (in particular the UK and the US) was exactly the opposite of what Phillips said should happen.

What went wrong? Why, after a century, did the Phillips Curve stop working? Two monetarist economists, Milton Friedman and Edmund Phelps, spotted the flaw with the Phillips Curve even before it broke down.

While the Phillips Curve happened to work well over a whole century, Friedman & Phelps said that it could only be relied on to work over short periods of time. To understand why, take a look at the explanation in the chart below. Imagine a government aims to reduce

Why the Phillips Curve did not work after the 1960s

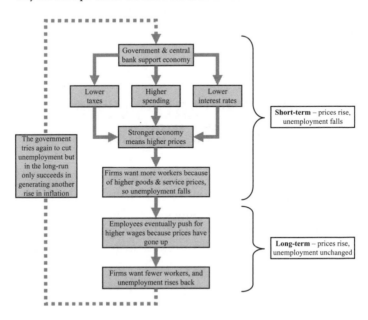

unemployment by introducing expansionary policies. This leads to stronger economic growth, in turn raising the prices of goods & services in the economy. With unchanged hourly wages, firms are happy to hire more workers because they are now getting more money for selling the product that their employees are making – and thus more profits. So, in the short-run, unemployment falls and we have higher inflation, just as Phillips suggested.

But workers will eventually realise that they are being duped – their hourly wage hasn't risen, but the cost of the goods & services they buy certainly has. So after a while they will demand higher wages – but we know that when wages rise firms want fewer workers, and unemployment goes back up again to where we started.

In the long run, therefore, Friedman and Phelps suggested that the only thing the government achieves by stimulating the economy is higher inflation, with no change in the number of workers. It would be impossible to keep unemployment below its natural rate because the government would have to continue boosting the economy by round after round of support, reducing unemployment only in the short-run and leading to ever higher rates of inflation. This is why the expansionary policies of the 1970s and the 1980s failed to reduce unemployment but caused rampant inflation.

Friedman and Phelps described the natural rate of unemployment in a different way to Phillips, therefore

– they called it the Non-Accelerating Inflation Rate of Unemployment, or for short the NAIRU. This might sound complicated but in reality it's not – it is just the underlying rate of unemployment that can be achieved in the economy without producing ever higher (this is the non-accelerating bit) rates of inflation. If inflation is kept unchanged then there should always be a tendency for unemployment to move back to this level.

The key policy implication of Friedman & Phelps' work is that a government cannot trade off unemployment and inflation in the long-run. Expansionary policies produce only a short term fall in unemployment below the natural rate until workers realised they have been conned by falling real wages (higher shop prices but no compensating change in nominal wages).

That's the theory, but how have unemployment and inflation actually moved together over recent decades? Taking the UK as an example, the following graph shows that while unemployment has moved up and down with the economic cycle, inflation has become less variable and generally lower over the past 15–20 years. This coincided with the Bank of England targeting inflation from 1993 onwards (and doing so as an independent body since 1997). In other words, inflation had to be kept stable whatever happened to unemployment.

The changing inflation/unemployment relationship in the UK

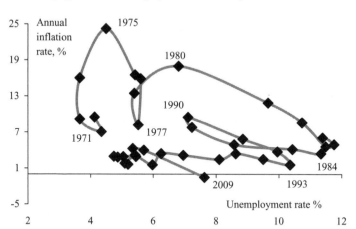

CHANGES IN THE WORKFORCE

In many countries labour markets have changed beyond recognition over the past few decades. To wrap up our exploration of the labour market we summarise below the main ways in which the market has altered:

▶ *Immigration.* Improved technology and transportation have 'globalised' labour markets around the world. From call centres located in Asia (so called 'offshoring') to the physical movement of workers from Eastern to Western Europe, the number of people able to provide their services to any country at any given time has increased dramatically. If employers in the UK, for example, know they can hire lower cost (and in some cases harder working) employees from abroad, then British workers will have to compete by accepting lower wages too. Increased availability of foreign workers has therefore introduced more competition, reduced bottlenecks and as a result cut firms' labour costs.

▶ *Manufacturing versus services.* As developed economies have increased their imports of lower-cost goods from abroad (particularly from Asia) domestic manufacturing industries have suffered and there has been a move to producing more services instead. This has led to a sharp decline in manufacturing employment in developed economies and a rise in manufacturing activity in developing countries. In the UK manufacturing jobs were more prevalent in the north of the country than the south, leading to a rise in structural unemployment in the north. And as we saw earlier in the chapter, the decline in certain industries often means that people are unemployed for longer periods as it takes time to retrain for, or relocate to, new jobs.

▶ *Part-time jobs & gender.* There has been a move towards more part-time employment in the UK, particularly as female participation in the labour market has increased. More and more women work following childbirth helped by changes in employment laws over the recent past, and because many new mothers prefer to work fewer hours the number of female part-time workers has risen – especially within the service sector. The proportion of people classified as self-employed (that is who run their own business) has also risen in the UK.

▶ *Ageing workforce.* Because of increased longevity in many countries people are now working until later in life to ensure they have adequate pensions to see them through their retirement. The credit crisis and the associated rise in government borrowing have meant that some governments have had to raise the retirement age to reduce state pension payments so they can balance their books. At the same time there are also fewer young people in the labour force as more students are staying on in education for longer than they did in the past. Even with a rise in the retirement age, the number of people who are not of working age (below 16 or above the retirement age) has risen sharply relative to the number of people of working age. This is known as the 'dependency ratio' as it tells us the proportion of workers who have to support the dependent or non-working population.

▶ *Government jobs.* In those countries where the scope of the government has been expanded over recent years, public sector employment has risen. In some cases, such as the UK, the increase in the number of government jobs has been sharp. In the aftermath of the credit crunch, as governments globally pare back their spending in an attempt to put their finances on a sounder footing, the number of people employed by the state could well fall too.

▶ *Trade unions.* Unions are no longer as important in the UK as they once were, thanks to the reforms enacted by Conservative governments in the 1980s and early 1990s. Employment and trade union laws were passed in 1980, 1982, 1984, 1988, 1989, 1990 and 1993 which limited the power of unions, made it easier for firms to hire and fire staff, and generally improved the flexibility of the market. As a result, the percentage of wage negotiations being bargained by unions has fallen, and so too has the level of classical unemployment.

What this shows us is that the market for jobs is ever changing. It has become much more flexible over recent years, as union power has been curtailed and firms have been able to more effectively tap into the global workforce. The market will continue to change in the future, with one of the most challenging aspects being how governments across the world adapt to ageing populations.

WHAT YOU NEED TO READ

▶ We have come across a lot of new definitions in this chapter, such as productivity, unemployment, the labour force, and the number of people active in the jobs market. The Organisation for Economic Cooperation and Development (OECD) provides a comprehensive glossary of economic terms here: *www.stats.oecd.org/glossary*.

▶ To get a feel for the sort of information on the UK jobs market that is published every month have a look at a UK labour market press release – but beware, it is 50 pages of pure statistics! *www.statistics.gov.uk/hub/labour-market*.

▶ One of the most comprehensive text books on the labour market currently in print is Richard Nickell, Stephen Layard, and Richard Jackman, *Unemployment: Macroeconomic Performance and the Labour Market*, Oxford University Press, 2005. However this is not for the faint hearted – it is a challenging read with lots of equations and charts.

IF YOU ONLY REMEMBER ONE THING

The number of people with jobs usually goes up and down with the economic cycle. But all economies have a certain amount of unemployment which won't go away however fast the economy is growing. Governments have learned – painfully in the 1970s and 1980s – that they can't simply accept higher inflation in exchange for lower unemployment. Sometimes, joblessness and high inflation can co-exist.

CHAPTER 4
TRADE

WHAT IT'S ALL ABOUT

- ► Why trade is beneficial for the global economy
- ► Why countries specialise in what they produce
- ► How the trade balance is made up of exports and imports
- ► How currencies can affect trade
- ► What the current account is
- ► Why governments use tariffs and quotas

WHAT IS INTERNATIONAL TRADE?

Walk into any supermarket in any country today and you will see an array of produce from around the world. There might be bananas from the Dominican Republic, green beans from Kenya or mangoes from India.

The same is true when you look on the roads. There will be cars from Germany, the United States and Japan to name a few. In fact, you will see the fruits of international trade in every part of daily life as modern technology and transport means more goods are being shipped around the world than ever before. There are toys made in China, shirts made in India, flat screen TVs in Korea and so on.

Trade, or the buying and selling of goods & services, is one of the foundation stones of all economies. Early societies may have relied on barter – the simple exchange of one good or service for another. Later, commodities like gold and silver were used as a form of payment and now, of course, we use money.

International trade is just the buying and selling of goods & services across national borders. It has also been going on for thousands of years. There is evidence of international trade routes going as far back as 3000 BC. The early Greeks would bring back spices from India. The Roman Empire created safe transportation routes so people could trade without fear of piracy.

So how is international trade different from trade within national borders? Perhaps the biggest difference is also its greatest advantage. It offers greater choice and provides a bigger market. If trade were restricted to just one country, then people would be limited to selling their goods in their home market. Think of the rush for Western companies to establish themselves in China. They are counting on being able to get a foothold selling into a market of more than 1 billion people. International trade also offers the chance to buy a bigger range of products. For example, people in France can now drink wine made in Spain, or Germany, or even New Zealand.

Another big difference is that international trade can be subject to greater regulation because it involves different countries. Each country regulates the flow of people, goods and money that passes across its borders. Within one country, it is usually relatively easy to move about or transport goods. But moving across borders is typically subject to immigration controls or customs.

In fact, some countries may throw up barriers to trade such as tariffs and quotas. The first is a tax on imported goods. The second is a limit on how much of a particular product can be brought into a country. Such measures are often referred to as examples of protectionism because countries introduce them to protect their own domestic industries or jobs.

Where the US gets its imports from

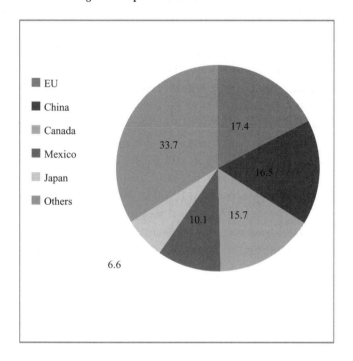

Of course, the other big difference between international and domestic trade is payment. Different countries or trading blocs tend to have their own currencies. People in the UK will have to exchange their pounds for euros if they want to buy wine from France. How many euros you get for one pound depends on the exchange rate set in foreign exchange markets. This relative price is also the result of trade flows between countries. For example, if people in the UK kept increasing the amount of wine they buy from France, they would then also need more euros. They would buy these with pounds, which would tend to push up the value of the euro against the pound.

International trade, of course, offers a much bigger marketplace but there are other reasons why countries trade with each other. The first is that different countries have different natural resources. Some countries may have very fertile farmland or have huge supplies of copper or gold. The Gulf states in the Middle East, for example, have oil. This is a very valuable commodity and many countries import their oil from these countries, making the oil exporters very rich in the process.

A second relates to difference in preferences. Even if countries had access to the same natural resources, they might trade with each other because they liked different things. For example, suppose the UK and France produce around the same amount of beer and wine. But the British like beer more and the French prefer wine. The British could sell their wine to the French and buy beer. Both sides would gain as a result.

One of the most important reasons for international trade, however, is the difference in costs. For example, salaries in China are much lower than they are in western countries. It is therefore much cheaper to manufacture goods in China which can then be sold at a lower price. That is why so much more manufacturing is now done

China's rising share of world trade

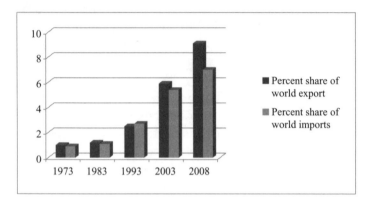

in countries like China or India and the goods they make exported to parts of the world where labour costs are higher.

Trade is also one of the surest ways out of poverty for many developing countries. This might be through the export of things like fruit and vegetables. Or it could be through manufactured goods utilising the cheaper labour that usually exists in those countries. Increased trade between countries is also likely to bind them together and reduce the likelihood of conflict.

While most economists preach the virtues of free international trade, some governments and special interest groups want to curtail trade if they feel it is costing jobs or hurting industries in their home countries. For example, India used to put very high duties on imported

WHO SAID IT

"No two countries that both had McDonald's had fought a war against each other since each got its McDonald's."
– Thomas Friedman

cars until the 1990s so that its consumers would buy cheaper domestically-made cars instead. In recent years, US politicians have been worried that cheap labour in China is driving production there and leading to the closure of factories in America.

COMPARATIVE ADVANTAGE

The English economist David Ricardo came up with perhaps the most persuasive argument about the benefits of international trade back in the 1800s. His principle of comparative advantage states that a country will benefit from producing and exporting any goods which it can make at a lower relative cost than other countries. Similarly, the country will stand to gain from importing a good that it makes relatively more expensively than other countries. What's more a country can gain from importing even if it can make those goods cheaper than anyone else.

The important concept here is what economists call opportunity cost. The opportunity cost of a good is the quantity of other goods that have to be sacrificed to produce another unit of that good. So according to the principle of comparative advantage, countries will gain when they export goods that have a lower opportunity cost than other countries.

Think of it like this. Imagine for simplicity's sake, there are only two countries – Country A and Country B. There are also only two types of goods – TVs and DVD players. It takes 30 hours of labour in Country A to make one TV and five hours to make a DVD player. In Country B, it takes 60 hours of labour to make one TV and six hours to make a DVD player.

On the face of it, Country A can make TVs and DVD players at less cost in terms of hours worked than Country B. That is what economists call absolute advantage and you would think there is no reason for Country A to trade.

But now think of it in terms of opportunity cost. Country A has to give up 6 DVD players for every TV it makes as that is the number it can make in the same time it makes a TV. But Country B has to sacrifice making 10 DVD players to make one TV.

So the opportunity cost of making a TV in Country A is 6 DVD players while the opportunity cost of making a TV in Country B is 10 DVD players. That shows that Country A has what economists call a comparative advantage in making TVs over Country B because it make them at a relatively lower cost.

Similarly, Country B has a comparative advantage in making DVD players because its opportunity cost for making one DVD player is 1/10 of a TV while the opportunity cost for Country A of making one DVD player is 1/6 of a TV.

So according to the principle of comparative advantage, Country A should specialise in making TVs and Country B should specialise in making DVD players. For example, if Country A makes 10 TVs, it has to give up 60 DVD players. But to make 60 DVD players, Country B only has to give up 6 TVs. So if both countries specialize, there

The principle of comparative advantage

	Hours needed to produce 1 unit	Opportunity cost
Country A		
TVs	30	6 DVD players
DVD player	5	1/6 of a TV
Country B		
TVs	60	10 DVD players
DVD players	6	1/10 of a TV

WHO YOU NEED TO KNOW
David Ricardo

David Ricardo's ideas have had a huge impact on economic thinking. The third of 17 children, Ricardo came from a Jewish family of Portuguese origin. He was born in London and followed his father to become a successful stockbroker. He amassed a huge personal fortune, in part by betting against a French victory at the Battle of Waterloo by investing in British securities.

Ricardo later became a member of parliament and started publishing papers on economics that still exert a massive influence on thinking to this day. He is perhaps best known for his theory of comparative advantage first advanced in his book *Principles of Political Economy*. According to the theory, even if one country could produce every good more efficiently than another country, it could still benefit by specialising in what it is best at producing. Ricardo's arguments are still used as a defence of free trade.

He also gave birth to the term Ricardian Equivalence – the theory that tax cuts today may have no effect on the economy now, because people will assume that they will have to pay for them in the future.

Ricardo also wrote widely on rent, wages and profits. For example, he stated that as real wages increase, real profits decrease because the revenue from the sale of manufactured goods is split between profits and wages.

can be extra TVs with no loss of DVD players. These are the gains of international trade.

It was in this way that Ricardo proved that all countries stood to gain from international trade even if one country had an absolute advantage in producing every good.

While Ricardo's model assumed that it was technological differences between countries that led to one having a comparative advantage over another, Swedish economists Eli Heckscher and Bertil Ohlin put forward a theory based on what economists call the factors of production of a country. These are the resources a country has available to make things, such as the amount of capital, labour or land. The Hecksher-Ohlin model, first developed in the 1930s, says that countries will export products that use their abundant factors of production and import those products that depend on scarce resources.

For example, India has a much bigger and cheaper workforce than the UK. The UK, however, has much more capital or machinery per worker so the relative cost of capital is cheaper. According to the Hecksher-Ohlin model then, it would make sense for the UK to specialise in making goods that were capital-intensive or required a lot of machinery. India, on the other hand, would be better off exporting goods which were much more labour-intensive as that's what it has in greater supply.

Of course, the world is not as simple as the two-country, two product models we've been looking at. Still, the principles can be extended to many countries. Just think of Country A as one country and Country B as the rest of the world. The concept can also be applied to many goods which are then arranged according to the comparative advantage of each.

There are, however, some more wrinkles as the theory of comparative advantage relies on assuming that there is a perfect market. In reality, prices and wages can take a lot of time to adjust. The model also takes no account of the business cycle – the notion that economies go up and down over a period of time. Nor does the model account for the effect on different people or sectors in the economy.

For example, a country might benefit overall from trade if it imports toys from another country where they are cheaply made. But that could still put the people who make toys in the first country out of business and they might not necessarily be able to transfer their skills to another industry. Still, the theory of comparative advantage to this day provides a useful benchmark for thinking about the benefits of international trade.

THE BALANCE OF PAYMENTS

Most modern economies are classed as open economies because they are open to international trade. One way of looking at how open they really are is to consider the total amount a country spends on imports as a proportion of its total spending (this of course took a knock during the financial crisis).

This brings us on to how economists keep track of what is going on with international trade. There are a variety of different items that together make up what is known as the balance of payments. First of all, you will hear about the trade balance. The trade balance is the value of exports minus imports. Statisticians tot up the value of all a country's exports and subtract that from the total value of imports. So if a country exports more than it imports, the trade balance will be positive. That is known as a trade surplus. The reverse of this is a trade deficit when the value of imports exceeds that of exports.

Economists also like to distinguish between the goods & services trade balance. The goods trade balance is relatively straightforward. It measures exports and imports of merchandise – this could include raw materials like oil or manufactured goods like toys and cars. The goods or merchandise items are also sometimes called visibles because you can see them – they are visible.

This differentiates them from the invisibles balance, which is made up mostly of trade in services. This consists of things like banking or insurance or even hairdressing and can, particularly in the modern world, form a very important part of international trade. For example, the UK has for several years run a goods trade deficit because it tends to import more goods than it exports. This is probably a consequence of a long-run decline in the importance of manufacturing. But it has tended to run a surplus on the services trade balance because of its banks and other financial services firms selling their services abroad.

In addition to the goods & services balance, the balance of payments also includes transfer payments. These are cash transactions which do not form payments for goods or services. Foreign aid to another country would be categorised as this. Another example is the payments European Union countries make to the running of the economic bloc's budget.

Then there is investment income which measures the earnings received on foreign investments less the earnings paid to foreigners on their investments in the home country. Together these four items (goods, services, income and transfers) make up what economists call the current account of the balance of payments. If the current account is in surplus, it means that a country's income exceeds its spending. If the current account is in deficit, then spending exceeds income.

The final piece of the balance of payments is the capital account. This is where economists record all international financial transactions. For example, if a UK company were to buy a French company, it would show up in the capital account. Japanese investors buying UK government bonds or company stocks would also be recorded in the capital account.

The sum of the capital and current accounts is called the balance of payments and technically should come to zero. Think of a current account surplus like a country's savings as it is the amount by which its international income exceeds its expenditure. A deficit, on the other hand, means there is a shortfall of cash. That money has to be either borrowed or paid for by the sale of assets. Either way, that should show up in the capital account which measures financial transactions.

Suppose the US has a current account deficit of $100 billion, perhaps because it is spending more on buying imports than it is on exporting. To plug the gap, it can either borrow that money or sell assets. Either of these will be recorded as a credit on the capital account because it brings money into the country.

That is why the current and capital account must sum to zero. Of course, in practice, they may not actually add up as such because of recording errors. The residual balance is often called a statistical discrepancy or balancing item.

You can see from the chart below how the balance of payments is made up. Adding together the goods & services balance together with transfer payments and investment income gives you the current account. The balancing item then makes sure the sum of the current account and the capital account comes to zero.

The balance of payments

	Trade in goods balance	-20
plus	Trade in services balance	4
plus	Transfer payments	2
plus	Investment income	6
equals	CURRENT ACCOUNT	-8
equals	CAPITAL ACCOUNT	5
plus	Balancing item	3
	BALANCE OF PAYMENTS	0

Financial markets tend to focus on both the goods trade balance numbers and the wider current account numbers because they can have a significant effect on exchange rates. Both can also be very politically sensitive. While the balance records a country's accounts with the rest of the world, the breakdown of the data released by statistics offices will often also show the position with individual countries. So, for example, we might want to look at the US-China bilateral trade balance, or the UK's trade balance with countries just in the European Union.

CURRENCIES AND TRADE

No discussion of trade would be complete without talking about currencies. Foreign exchange rates strongly affect, and are strongly affected by, a country's trading patterns. Payment in different currencies is a defining feature of most international trade outside of currency blocs like the euro zone where all countries use the same currency – in this case, the euro.

The foreign exchange rate is the price of one currency against another currency. Suppose there's a UK company importing wine from France. It needs to know how many euros it will get for its pounds and the French company needs to know how many pounds it will get for its euros.

Now suppose the exchange rate starts off with one pound buying 1.50 euros and a bottle of French wine costs 5 euros. It will cost the UK company £3.33. Suppose the pound goes up in value – it appreciates. It now buys 1.75 euros. This means that the UK company will be able to get the same bottle of wine for £2.85. The bottle of wine has become cheaper for the UK company. It can get more wine for the same money, thereby pushing up international demand for French wine. Now suppose instead the pound goes down in value, or depreciates, to 1.25 euros. That makes the bottle of wine more expensive (£4) and will thus lower international demand for French wine.

You can see from the above example that the exchange rate can have a real effect on demand for traded goods. When the value of a country's currency goes up, it makes imported goods cheaper, increasing demand for them. But if the currency goes down, then imports became more expensive eventually and so less desirable. Similarly, a country will see demand for its exports go up when its currency weakens and vice versa.

So a fall in a country's exchange rate should push the surplus higher or deficit lower because it cuts imports and raises exports. A rise in the exchange rate, on the other hand, should raise the deficit or lower the surplus because it raises imports and cuts exports.

Sterling's exchange rate with the US dollar since 1975

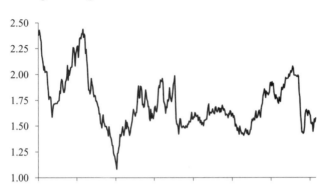

GOING BACK TO BALANCE

Most advanced economies like the UK and US have what economists call floating exchange rates. That means their value is set by supply and demand without government intervention. Some countries, however, opt for what is known as a fixed exchange rate. Under a fixed exchange regime, the government or the central bank is committed to maintaining a particular rate or range for its currency against another currency.

It will thus buy and sell its currency to try to preserve that rate. So if people were selling its currency so much that its value would fall below the fixed rate, then the central bank would step in and buy as much of the currency needed so it stayed at the fixed rate.

Of course, there are times when it might not be feasible for the government to maintain a fixed exchange rate despite its intervention. In September, 1992, Britain was a member of the European Exchange Rate Mechanism (ERM) – the system of fixed exchange rates that preceded the launch of the euro in 1999. That meant the pound's value was fixed to other currencies in the ERM. But traders in foreign exchange markets kept selling the pound because they were not convinced the fixed exchange rate would stick, forcing its value down. The Bank of England spent billions trying to defend the value of the pound but in the end the government had to admit defeat and pull out of the ERM.

Finally, some countries may also adopt what is known as a dirty or managed float of their currency. In this regime, the government or the central bank may regularly intervene in the foreign exchange markets, perhaps to stop its currency rising too much and hurting the prospects of its exporters, but there is no set rate.

We saw earlier how the value of the exchange rate can affect the trade balance or the current account. But the trade balance and current account can also have significant effects on the exchange rate.

Imagine there are only two countries – the US and Japan. Both countries have their own exchange rates – the dollar and the yen. Now suppose the US is running a trade deficit so its imports from Japan exceed its exports to Japan. US companies need to sell more dollars to get yen than Japanese companies need dollars to pay for their imports of American goods. This means there is an excess supply of dollars and an excess demand for yen. As we have seen a number of times already, the price of everything is determined by supply and demand. So it should come as no surprise that the value of the dollar should fall against the yen.

In brief: if a country runs a current account deficit, its currency should depreciate or fall in value because it implies there is an excess of its currency available as money leaving the country is outstripping that coming in. Similarly, if a country is running a surplus, its currency should appreciate or rise in value.

In economic theory, in a world of floating exchange rates, this should ultimately restore deficits and surpluses to balance. To see this let's return to our example of the US and Japan. The fall in the value of the dollar will make imports from Japan more expensive. The US will therefore cut the amount it imports. At the same time, its exports to Japan will have become cheaper. Japan should increase the amount of US exports it buys. This will reduce the trade deficit until it comes into balance.

In reality, however, life is much more complicated. Firms may take a long time to adjust the amount of goods they buy or sell because of changes in the exchange rate. In fact, it is possible that if a currency depreciates, the trade balance will initially fall. This is because the immediate effect of the currency depreciating is to make imports more expensive and exports will sell for less foreign currency while their volumes initially remain the same.

Economists call this effect the J-curve (the graph below) as the trade balance initially dips when the currency falls but then starts rising as firms adjust the amount of imports and exports being bought and sold.

The effects of a currency change: The J curve

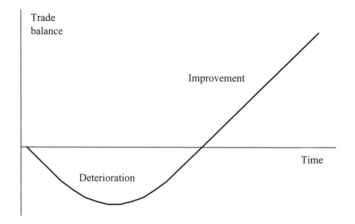

Firms may also try and offset their exposure to fluctuating currencies by hedging. This involves taking a position in one market to protect against losses in another. Firms may, for instance, lock in an exchange rate for a transaction to occur in the future – this is known as a forward contract.

Moreover, the value of the currencies in the modern world is set in the global foreign exchange market where a few trillion dollars are traded every working day. Traders operating in giant financial institutions can buy and sell securities from around the world at the touch of a button.

Given this, changes in the value of the exchange rate tend to be driven much more by financial transactions. Suppose a US bank wants to buy stock in Japanese companies. It will need yen to do this and so will sell dollars in exchange. The effect will be to lower the dollar versus the yen.

Nowadays, freely moving capital around the world means that countries can run current account deficits indefinitely as long as the gaps are being financed by a surplus on the capital account.

The United States is a good example of this. It has been running a current account deficit for a long time as its imports vastly exceed its exports. In one respect, it is living beyond its means. Now you might expect this situation would result in there being an excess supply of dollars available on the market, which would then push the US currency down.

The US current account deficit as a percentage of GDP

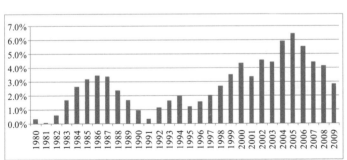

But remember the financial account is the mirror image of the current account. People outside the US, most notably China, are using their surplus money to buy US Treasuries, essentially IOUs from the US government. Current account surplus countries like China therefore are financing the US current account deficit.

PURCHASING POWER PARITY

Exchange rates may be set by supply and demand but how do we know what a fair value is for any currency? Economists like to use a concept called purchasing power parity (PPP) to assess the relative value of currencies. This looks at the buying power of a currency so if an item cost £10 in the UK and $20 in the US, a fair exchange rate should be $2 to the pound, according to PPP theory, which, of course, looks not just at one pair of prices but lots of them.

In reality, however, the prices of the same good can vary wildly across different countries depending on its supply, the demand for it, the cost of production, consumer incomes, etc. Prices can even vary significantly between regions in the same country or even city. For example, the price of a meal out will tend to be much higher in London than in the north of England as restaurateurs have to make up for things like higher rents and labour costs.

To get round this, the Economist magazine reports the Big Mac index. This looks at the cost of a McDonald's hamburger across the world to come up with an assessment of a fair value for the currency on the assumption that the Big Mac is a generic good that is available internationally.

So if a Big Mac cost $3 in the US and £2 in the UK, then the exchange rate can be determined as £1 equals $1.50. However, even this approach has limitations because while McDonald's' hamburgers are considered a cheap fast food in most Western countries, they are more of a luxury item in some developing countries. For example, in India, McDonald's' restaurants are usually only found in upmarket shopping areas and its clientele tends to be affluent young people.

THE ASIAN CRISIS

We saw earlier that a country can run a current account or trade deficit for a while as long as foreign investors are willing to finance that deficit by lending it money. That does mean, however, that countries can become reliant on that funding. The US therefore needs China to keep buying its government bonds. If China stopped buying US securities, the result could be a drop in the value of the dollar.

The Asian financial crisis in 1997 is a lesson of what happens when capital flows dry up. Thailand then became a victim of what economists refer to as a balance of payments or currency crisis.

All through the early 1990s, Asian economies like Thailand, Korea and Indonesia had been doing spectacularly well and growing strongly. But they had also been running big current account deficits while unofficially fixing their currencies to the dollar. Through that time they witnessed strong capital inflows as they looked abroad to finance expansion.

As their exchange rates were fixed to the dollar, the Asian economies were able to benefit from the weakness of the US currency in the early 1990s. That meant they were weaker against the Japanese yen, the main trading currency of the region and thus able to boost their share of exports. But when the trend in the dollar changed in 1995, they found their currencies appreciating against the yen, cutting their share of trade at a time when their current account deficits were already running high.

Capital flows began to fall as higher interest rates in the US started attracting more money there. The Thai currency, which was fixed to the dollar, was under particular downward pressure from speculators. The authorities then had to raise interest rates themselves to stop money flowing out of the economy. This damaged the economy further and increased bankruptcies until the authorities could no longer maintain the fixed exchange rate to the dollar in July 1997.

The result was an instant fall in the value of the currency. That meant the foreign debt they had was even more costly in terms of the domestic currency, triggering more defaults and bankruptcies. The crisis then spread to other Asian countries, leading to a number of currencies losing as much as half their value.

The International Monetary Fund (IMF) established bailout packages for the stricken countries but demanded tough conditions such as higher interest rates to restore confidence in the domestic currency. These measures were regarded as controversial as some economists argued they exacerbated the recessions in those countries.

PROTECTIONISM

The Asian crisis led to many people criticising speculators in financial markets. Blame was laid at the door of so-called 'hot money' that flowed freely from one capital market to another. Some people argued that greater controls should be put in place to prevent such volatile flows.

True or not, recessions or crises often lead to calls for protectionism in trade policy. While economists may argue that trade and open markets are beneficial to the world economy as a whole, it may well be the case that not everyone gains. For example, Americans may benefit from cheaper clothes made in China but factory workers who used to make those clothes in the US may lose their jobs.

Governments, therefore, often put in place restrictions to protect particular industries or groups. The most common of these is a tariff or import duty. By imposing a tax on certain imported goods, governments can make them more expensive in the hope that it will cut demand for the import and shift it to the domestically-produced good.

WHO YOU NEED TO KNOW
Paul Krugman

University of Princeton professor Paul Krugman grew up in New York and studied at the University of Yale before getting his PhD from the Massachusetts Institute of Technology in 1977. He has taught there as well as the London School of Economics, Stanford and the University of California at Berkeley.

The author of 20 books, Krugman also writes a regular column in the *New York Times* on current economic and political issues. His blog is also very widely read, making him one of the best-known modern-day economists.

Krugman won the Nobel Prize in 2008 for his contribution to international trade theory. He argued that Ricardo's theory of comparative advantage, where each country specialises in producing the item that it can make relatively cheaper, did not fully capture the reasons for production in international trade. He argued that brand preferences also played a part and that countries would produce those things which afforded them economies of scale – that is mass production became cheaper for them.

During the 1997 Asian crisis, Krugman advocated currency controls as a way to mitigate the crisis. Only Malaysia followed that course and its government has credited the policy with helping it through the crisis. Krugman was also a stern critic of former US president George W. Bush. His best-selling book, *The Great Unravelling*, argued that the large deficits of the Bush administration in the early 2000s were unsustainable and would eventually generate a major economic crisis.

For example, India imposes a duty of above 100% on imported wine and spirits. That means if a bottle of whisky normally cost the equivalent of £10, duty would add at least another £10. This makes imported spirits in India very expensive compared with domestically-produced liquor. Consumers therefore are likely to choose the Indian-made spirits over imports, protecting domestic jobs and firms.

Arguments made in favour of tariffs often include that they are needed to protect particular ways of life or crafts-manship; that they nurture fledgling industries; and that they ensure scarce resources in poor countries are not frittered away on luxury items. However, if every country tried to protect their domestic industry, there would be less international trade and the world economy would be the loser.

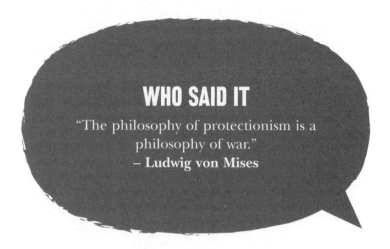

WHO SAID IT

"The philosophy of protectionism is a philosophy of war."
– Ludwig von Mises

Quotas are another form of protectionist trade policy. In this case, there is a limit, or quota, put on the amount of a good that can be imported. This also has the effect of raising the domestic price of the imported good because its supply has been restricted. For example, the European Union has ceilings on poultry imports.

Another example of how imports may be restricted is the existence of non-tariff barriers. These may be things like delays clearing imports through customs which make them less attractive. The government may ask for goods to meet particular specifications that foreign producers may be less aware of or unable to match.

Governments may also try and support their exporters through subsidies. These are grants or other government assistance to domestic firms who are competing with foreign firms. This has the effect of lowering the price the domestic firm can charge so as to make it more competitive against foreign firms. The European Union's Common Agricultural Policy is an example of such a subsidy.

Exchange rate management may be another way that governments can boost their exports or cut down on imports. For example, China has a fixed exchange rate to the dollar. Many US politicians have argued that the Chinese have unfairly benefited by keeping the rate of their currency lower than it should be, thereby boosting Chinese exports.

So what stops governments from always using tariffs, quotas or subsidies to help their own economies? In fact, there was a school of thought known as Mercantilism which flourished in Europe from the 16th to the 18th centuries that believes that governments should restrict imports and encourage exports. Well, if everyone put up barriers to trade, there would be no trade left. Trade wars would make the global economy a poorer place.

GLOBAL TRADE DEALS

This is where the World Trade Organisation (WTO) comes in. It officially came into being in 1995 when it replaced the General Agreement on Tariffs and Trade (GATT) which had been set up after World War Two. Its purpose is to create the rules for the multilateral trading system through a system of agreements that are signed up to by the majority of the world's economies. It has more than 150 member countries and covers 97% of world trade.

Since 2001, the WTO has been trying to clinch a global trade deal called the Doha Round after the Qatari city where the initial meeting took place. The avowed purpose is to spread the benefits of globalisation to poorer countries and break down trade barriers. The debate has been very contentious, however, with developed and developing countries finding it difficult to establish common ground on a variety of issues such as agricultural subsidies in the rich world.

Global imbalances are another issue which policymakers have been unable to come up with a satisfactory solution to. By this they mean that certain countries like the US have big current account deficits which are then matched by equally large current account surpluses in countries like China.

Many economists say this is a situation that can't go on indefinitely and makes the world more susceptible to crises as it is overly reliant on the US consumer. So far, however, there has been little progress in tackling the imbalances which have become a feature of the world economy for more than a decade.

Despite these concerns, international trade continues to improve the lives of billions of people on the planet by increasing the overall wealth in the global economy. For many countries, it remains the only route out of poverty and the remarkable advance of economies like India and China shows just how powerful a force it can be.

WHAT YOU NEED TO READ

▶ The World Trade Organisation has a comprehensive website discussing its aims and has articles on live issues in international trade: *www.wto.org/*.

▶ For a scathing criticism of the policy failures of organisations like the International Monetary Fund and their role in the Asian crisis, read *Globalization and Its Discontents* by former World Bank chief economist Joseph Stiglitz, WW Norton and Co, 1996.

▶ Nobel Prize-winning economist Paul Krugman has a provocative blog where he regularly discusses international trade and other economic policy issues: *www.krugman.blogs.nytimes.com/*.

▶ Economist David Ricardo's original 1817 work *On the Principles of Political Economy and Taxation* is still an incredibly elegant exposition of his trade and other economic theories. Prometheus Books, 1996.

▶ For an interesting take on the emergence of China as the big economic superpower, try *China Inc* by Ted C. Fishman, Simon and Schuster, 2005.

IF YOU ONLY REMEMBER ONE THING

International trade is the buying and selling of goods between different countries. The trade balance is the difference between exports and imports. A country can run a current account deficit as long as other countries are willing to finance that deficit.

CHAPTER 5
MONEY

WHAT IT'S ALL ABOUT

- ► Why money exists and how we measure it
- ► What affects how much money people hold
- ► Where money comes from and how banks can 'create' it
- ► The relationship between money, activity and inflation
- ► Who is borrowing and who is saving money
- ► The importance of borrowing to the economy and the credit crunch

WHY DOES MONEY EXIST?

This might sound an odd question to begin with. Surely it's obvious what money is – it's the notes and coins we carry around in our back pockets to buy goods & services in the shops, as well as the money we keep in our bank accounts. While that's true, there happens to be a lot more to defining money.

It wasn't always like this, being able to whip out a £20 note or a credit or debit card to pay for what you wanted. Before money existed we used to trade with each other by a system of barter – offering something you have in return for someone else's belongings. The problem with this system was what was called the 'double coincidence of wants' – not only do you need to find a person who has what you want, but to get it he or she must want what you have to offer.

Thus, one of the four key functions of money is it operates as a 'medium of exchange'. The second purpose of money is that it is a 'unit of account', allowing us to judge the price of goods & services by the same standard – in other words, in terms of US dollars in the United States, pounds sterling in the UK and euros in Europe. Thirdly it is a 'store of value' – we can earn money now and keep it to spend at a later date. When an economy has high inflation it can undermine this function because money becomes worth less in terms of the goods & services it can buy over time. Finally, money is 'standard of deferred payment', which simply means that we can settle future debts with it (which is a similar function to the store of value).

In the past money itself used to be actually worth something – the materials that were used to create coins were things like gold and silver which had intrinsic value. The problem with this was that people used to cheat the system by either 'clipping' (trimming the coins) or 'debasement' (recreating coins with a lower gold or silver content).

We've come a long way since then. One of the reasons that this system was replaced by paper money was that it was cumbersome to carry around heavy gold coins. So instead, people began depositing their heavy gold with banks, and in return received receipts which promised to repay the bearer that particular gold deposit in the future. These notes could then be used to pay

A gold receipt

for goods & service more practically than by using the gold itself.

There was one more crucial step on the way from this system becoming what we know today. The banks that held the gold deposits on behalf of their owners realised that it was a shame to have such a big stock of gold doing nothing, especially when very few of the owners cashed in their receipts at any given time. So what they began to do was issue more receipts than the gold they were looking after – in other words, they loaned the gold to people who wanted to borrow it. As long as people with receipts didn't all demand the gold back at the same time the system would work.

It wasn't that long ago since *countries* operated this system – the 'gold standard', whereby governments promised to exchange money for gold at a predefined rate (even though they didn't have enough gold to satisfy all of the notes they had issued), existed until the early 1970s.

What operates now is a system called 'fiat money'. The notes and coins in your pocket and the money balances in your bank accounts are intrinsically not worth anything, and can't be converted into gold at some predefined rate. Rather, people place their trust in the central bank that it will not issue excess amounts of money – otherwise it could become worthless in the future through higher prices. This is the reason that achieving low and stable inflation is so important.

WHAT IS MONEY TODAY?

Most countries produce monthly figures on the amount of money in the economy. We can define what we call money in a number of ways, starting off from a very narrow measure of notes and coins to very broad measures which include various types of bank deposit. These various measures are labelled M0 all the way through to M4, as the graph below shows. These are not always exactly the same in each country – what we have done in the graph below is to look at what are the most common definitions used across the world.

Definitions of money

NARROW MONEY

M0 – narrow or base money
equals notes and coins in circulation or in bank tills plus banks' reserve balances held at the central bank

M1
equals M0 plus money held in cheque and other no-notice accounts (both retail & wholesale)

M2
equals M1 plus money held in savings accounts and short-notice wholesale funds

M3
equals M2 plus longer term bank deposits and tradable wholesale bank accounts (CDs)

M4
equals M3 plus even longer term deposits and commercial paper/short term bonds

BROAD MONEY

VERY LIQUID

LESS LIQUID

The narrowest measure of money is what's called the 'monetary base', also referred to as M0. This is made up of all the notes and coins in circulation among the public, money in banks' tills, and the cash deposits (known as reserves) held by commercial banks with the central bank. People tend to hold notes and coins for everyday use when buying goods & services, but given the increased use of credit and debit cards the relative size (and relevance) of narrow money has fallen over recent years.

As a result, there is usually a lot more focus on the broader measures of money, such as M3 and M4, which include less liquid (in other words less easily accessible) deposits held in savings accounts. These are the sort of deposits we might have to give the bank some notice before they can be withdrawn. These measures also include things like certificates of deposit (or CDs), which are essentially bank balances traded in the financial (or wholesale) markets. M4 includes commercial paper and bonds, which are IOUs issued by firms (and, in the case of bonds, the government).

The speed with which money holdings in an economy grow is important because it can provide clues about the health of the economy. In turn, that could influence the rate of inflation so central banks – most of which try to control inflation – pay particularly close attention to money. Very few central banks publish the full array of money definitions as shown in the previous graph, with the European Central Bank (ECB) focusing most closely on M3, the Bank of England on M4 and the US Federal Reserve on M1 and M2.

When people change their preferences for how long they want to tie their money up in bank accounts this can change the amount of money in each of the measures we've looked at above. For example, if people decided to move their money from low interest current accounts to higher paying notice accounts there would be no impact on broad money (because it includes both) but narrower money holdings should fall.

MONEY DEMAND – THE MOTIVES FOR HOLDING MONEY

So, we've talked about the various different measures of money, but who holds all of this money and why? The main holders of money in the private sector are individuals, firms, and financial service providers such as banks. The government too holds money balances in the form of the tax revenues it generates, which are ultimately redistributed through the economy when it pays that money out – in benefits, for example.

There are three main motives for households to hold money – as originally identified by John Maynard Keynes back in the 1930s. First, there is the transactions motive. People keep cash in their wallets/purses and money in their bank accounts so that they can make everyday purchases or save up for larger items. Second is the precautionary motive. This is the money people set aside just in case something unexpected crops up. And finally there is the speculative motive. You may want to hold your wealth in the form of money because you're worried about making a financial loss by holding other assets like a house or shares (both of which are less liquid than money – in other words, they take longer to turn into hard cash).

MONEY SUPPLY AND CREDIT CREATION

That's the *demand* for money, but where does it come from? In other words, what about the *supply*? Well, the easy answer is that governments and central banks can increase the quantity of money in an economy if they wish by simply printing or minting more notes and coins – we'll learn more about that later in the book in the chapter on central banking. But that's only half the story.

The government/central bank is not the only source of money supply. Don't forget that when we looked at the various types of money earlier in the chapter we saw that it could be held either as physical notes or coins, or electronically in the form of bank accounts. And it turns out that the amount of money held in bank accounts can also be expanded – even if the central bank keeps the physical quantity of notes and coins the same. How is it that banks can create money at the stroke of a pen or (these days) a push of a button?

When banks take in deposits from people and firms in an economy they don't keep much of those deposits readily accessible. A bit like the banks we encountered at the start of this chapter that took in gold deposits, modern day banks have learnt that not everyone will want their money back at the same time. What they do, therefore, is to keep a very small portion of that deposited money – typically less than 5% – available to pay back if needed (this is called the bank's 'reserve ratio'), and lend out the rest of it. After all, what's the point of leaving all that money sitting around doing nothing when it could be lent out and earning interest?

For sake of simplicity assume that the bank keeps 10% of each depositor's money in its tills doing nothing and lends out the remaining 90%. A new customer depositing £100 with the bank would thus lead to an extra £90 of on-lending by the bank. But the money which is lent out by the bank is then spent by the borrower, perhaps at a shop. The shopkeeper then deposits his extra £90 of takings at the end of the day with his bank, which then does exactly the same – it keeps 10% of it (£9) and lends out the other 90% (£81).

This process keeps on going and going, and by the time it is complete there have been a total of £1000 of new deposits created, including the initial deposit (that is, £100 + £90 + £81 + £73 + £66 ...) – all generated from one person going into his bank and depositing £100 to begin with. And the smaller is the reserve ratio, the larger the amount of money that banks can 'create' this way. Try it for yourself – instead of assuming the bank keeps 10% of its deposits try 5% and you should find that from an initial deposit of £100 money in the economy will expand to £2000 (including the initial £100). Because bank deposits are money, money has been created by the simple process of deposits being lent by the bank. The amount by which money increases relative to the size of the initial deposit (in these cases by factors of 10 and 20) is called the money multiplier.

The money multiplier (10% reserve ratio)

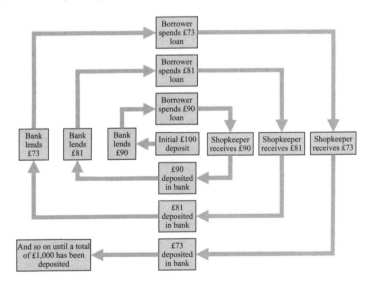

What money creation does is to expand the balance sheets of banks. The balance sheet just tells us how much the bank has taken in as deposits – its liabilities – and how much is owed to the bank in outstanding customer loans – its assets. In the example above, banks as a whole have taken in an extra £1000 of deposit liabilities, matched by increased assets of £900 lending and £100 cash in tills.

One point worth making here is that the multiplier can and does change significantly over time – it is not constant. For example, when banks scaled back on their lending during the credit crunch the multiplier collapsed.

WHO SAID IT

"The process by which banks create money is so simple that the mind is repelled."
– **John Kenneth Galbraith**

HOW INTEREST RATES ARE DETERMINED

It turns out that money plays a key role in influencing the rate of interest in the economy. To understand how, we need to think of money separately from other assets like shares, bonds and houses. Consider a relatively narrow or liquid measure of money – cash holdings and money held in short-notice bank accounts – as this is what most people would describe as being money anyway. These typically pay either zero or close to zero interest because they are so liquid – i.e. available to be used at very short notice.

Now, imagine that interest rates in the economy as a whole are too high. In other words, government and corporate bonds (IOUs promising to repay lenders a certain amount at a fixed date in the future) are offering very good rates of return. Would you want to hold your money in a short-notice bank account? The answer of course is no – while you wouldn't actually be losing anything by leaving your money in a bank, you would be missing out on a better return somewhere else. This is a concept that economists refer to as 'opportunity cost'. The reverse is also true – if interest rates in the economy were too low, then you may prefer to keep your wealth in the form of cash because you're not losing out that much by doing so.

In reality, the demand for money will be dependent on lots of things, such as how much people earn and the prices of goods & services – as both will influence the amount of money people hold in order to buy things. But when it comes to interest rates, people usually want to hold more money the lower is the rate of interest. This is shown by the downward sloping line in the graph below. The interest rate should settle at a level which makes people hold precisely the fixed amount of money that is available in the economy at any given time.

How interest rates are determined

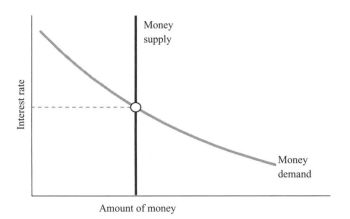

Amount of money

THE QUANTITY THEORY OF MONEY

How the amount of money in an economy changes can have an important bearing on the how quickly economic activity expands and how fast prices rise. The

Quantity Theory

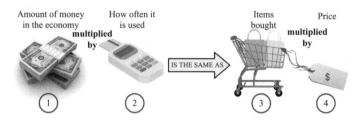

Amount of money in the economy — multiplied by — How often it is used — IS THE SAME AS — Items bought — multiplied by — Price

1   2   3   4

relationship between money and nominal GDP (in other words the value of spending) in an economy is called the Quantity Theory of Money. What it says is this: the amount of spending on goods & services in an economy each year must equal the amount of money there is in that economy multiplied by the average number of times it's used during the year. As an example, imagine a very small economy in which there was just one £20 note, and that this note was used twice during the year. It must be the case, then, that the value of goods & services bought during the year was £40. The number of times money is used – or the speed with which it moves around between people and firms (in the above example twice) – is rather aptly called the 'velocity of circulation'.

We can show this pictorially in the diagram above, which is known as the 'equation of exchange'. The reason that the Quantity Theory is so important is because it helps us understand what happens to an economy when the amount of money changes. Imagine the speed with which money is passed round the economy – or velocity (labelled 2 in the diagram above) – doesn't change. More money

(1) must then lead to a rise in the right hand side of our picture above – in other words the amount spent on goods & services in the economy (3 times 4). This higher spending must mean one of two things (or some combination of both):

1. A rise in the number of goods & services bought (3) but no change in prices (4)
2. No change in the number of goods & services bought (3) but a rise in prices (4)

WHO YOU NEED TO KNOW
Irving Fisher

Irving Fisher is best known for his work on money, interest rates and their impact on the economy. He was the first economist to distinguish between *nominal* interest rates (the usual deposit and lending rates that you see advertised by banks and other financial institutions) and *real* interest rates. The real interest rate is the nominal rate after taking account of inflation in an economy. So, if nominal deposit interest rates were 5% and inflation was 2%, then the real rate would be 3%. In this example we'd be able to buy 3% more goods & services if we saved up for a year. Fisher described the failure to take into consideration the rate of inflation when making economic decisions as 'money illusion'.

For him, money illusion was responsible for the cyclical ups and downs in the economy. A rise in both nominal interest rates and inflation by the same amount would leave real interest rates unchanged, so while it would be more costly for businesses to borrow for investment, they would at the same time get more money for their products they sell. But firms might not realise this, their money illusion leading to a reduction in the amount they borrow and the start of a downswing in the economy.

Fisher also thought about how the demand for and supply of funds would influence interest rates. The demand for funds will depend on productivity – the more productive are a firm's investments, the more they will want to borrow money to invest. The supply of funds depends on how much households are willing to save, which in turn depends on how much they want to spend now versus save for the future. The interest rate should move to a level where both the suppliers of funds and those wanting them are happy.

The Quantity Theory of Money which we have looked at in detail in this chapter owes its existence to Irving Fisher who first wrote down the 'equation of exchange' shown in the graph above back in 1911.

Monetarist economists usually argue that increasing the amount of money in the economy affects neither the average number of times it is used (2) nor the number of goods & services bought (3), so that a rise in money must lead directly to a rise in prices in the economy (4). Another way of putting this is that allowing the quantity of money to expand will cause inflation. After all, if people are holding more money than they would like, one way to resolve this is to spend it – which has the effect of driving prices higher. This is theory that is behind one of the most famous recent-day economists' – Milton Friedman's – view of the world.

WHO SAID IT

"Inflation is always and everywhere a monetary phenomenon."
– Milton Friedman

THE IMPORTANCE OF MONEY IN PRACTICE

We've looked at the theory, now let's take a look at the relationship between money, activity and inflation in the real world. The graph below shows that broad money in the UK has generally tracked up and down reasonably closely with both inflation and nominal GDP over a long period of time. The relationships are not perfect, however

Money, inflation and economic activity

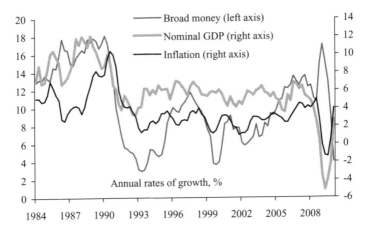

– it is not always easy to tell how inflation will move as a result of a change in the money supply. To quote Milton Friedman once again, the time lags between changes in the money supply and inflation can be 'long and variable'.

We've looked at the relationship between money and inflation over time, but what does it look like across countries? We'd expect that those countries with the highest rate of money growth are also the ones with the highest rates of inflation, based on what we've learnt so far in this chapter. It turns out that this is true – take a look at the scatter plot of the graph below, which shows that over a period of 10 years there is a clear positive relationship between money growth and inflation.

Money and inflation in selected advanced economies over the past decade

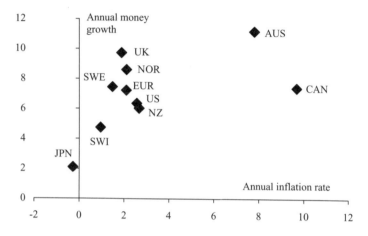

So it's understandable that governments and central banks in the past have attempted to control the money supply in the hope that this would in turn limit inflation. Probably the best example of this was the UK 30 years ago. Back in 1980 the recently elected Thatcher government laid out what was called the Medium Term Financial Strategy – or MTFS for short. Targets for various measures of the money supply were set, which formed the basis for monetary policy decisions. In particular, the way the Bank of England (which at that point in time was not independent of the government, as it is now) attempted to control money growth was by raising interest rates. That would be expected to limit the demand for loans – as it would be more expensive to borrow – and therefore the rate at which banks create money.

This strategy was eventually dropped in 1986 because it was proving too difficult to achieve. Remember that central banks control directly only a portion of the money supply – that of base money, or M0, through its printing operations. Money creation by commercial banks was difficult to restrict – especially when the government was simultaneously trying to liberalise the banking system from the regulatory straightjacket that it had previously operated within.

Central banks these days generally no longer target the money supply, but instead the rate of inflation directly. That said, money remains a highly important indicator that policymakers monitor closely. During the recent recession interest rates were cut to such low levels in many countries that the only policy option left available to central banks was to directly increase base money in the hope that people would spend it, thereby stimulating economic activity. This was done by the European Central Bank, the Bank of England and US Federal Reserve among others. We will look more closely at this so called policy of 'quantitative easing' alongside the operation of monetary policy more generally in the chapter on central banks.

THE BORROWERS AND SAVERS OF MONEY

So far we've learnt that financial intermediaries such as banks take in deposits from various sources – such as households and firms – who have sufficient cash, and then lend it out to those who need to borrow. In fact, as we saw, they usually lend a lot more out than they have in hard cash.

In our money creation example above the banks themselves are just the intermediaries, or middlemen. They are neither *net* borrowers nor lenders, because their financial assets (the loans they have made along with the cash in their tills) are equal to their liabilities (the money they owe to the people who have deposited money with them). It is households who are *net borrowers* (they've borrowed money and used it to purchase goods & services) while the shops are *net savers* or *lenders* of money. Effectively, in our example it was the shopkeepers that financed households' borrowing, with the banks operating as the go-between.

Who is doing the borrowing and lending in the real world? After all, economies are made up of more than just the banks, shops and households that we looked at in the example above. To begin with, we can list the main groups or sectors within an economy which might be borrowing and lending money:

- ▶ Households
- ▶ Private non-financial firms
- ▶ Private financial firms (such as banks)
- ▶ The government
- ▶ The rest of the world

A sector as a whole is a net borrower if the total amount of money being borrowed by some in that sector is more than the total amount others have saved. Conversely, the sector is a net saver (or lender) of money if the amount of money saved is greater than the amount borrowed.

We can illustrate this by thinking about households. Some will be saving money, perhaps for a deposit on a house or because they've paid off their mortgage and have spare cash to put aside. Other households, however, will be borrowing money, perhaps because they don't have enough money of their own sitting around to buy a car or a house.

While any sector can be an overall borrower or saver, the amount of borrowing *in total* must be equal to the amount of saving. Put simply, borrowers must get their money from somewhere – for each extra pound borrowed there must be an extra pound saved somewhere in the world.

HOUSEHOLD BORROWING AND DEBT

So far we have looked at the amount of borrowing and saving in an economy, and the sectors which are doing it. It is important, however, to distinguish between the amount of money that people borrow in any given period (say a year) and the total amount of debt that they hold – that is, the cumulative amount of borrowings to date which have not yet been paid back.

Following the onset of the credit crisis in 2007, house-holds in many developed economies either stopped bor-rowing or couldn't borrow money. That's not to say no households at all borrowed money; rather that more were paying down their debt than were taking on more debt. Even though *borrowing* came to a standstill, house-holds in many countries had accumulated a vast amount of *debt* over the previous decade, largely the result of higher house prices and therefore mortgages. In fact, according to OECD figures, UK households owed more money relative to the amount of income they earned than households in any other G7 economy at the end of the first decade of the twenty-first century.

Household debt relative to incomes

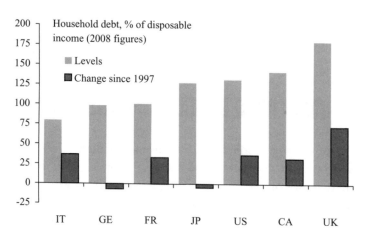

Just like any other debtors households must pay interest on their outstanding stock of debt. In many countries, by far the largest amount of debt racked up by households over recent years has been mortgages. In the UK, for example, mortgages account for about 85% of all household debt, with the remaining 15% being consumer credit (think car loans, credit cards, store cards and the like).

But the type of interest rate that households face varies significantly from country to country. In the UK, for example, while mortgage loans are paid back over a long period of time, the interest rate at which they are paid tends to change quite regularly. Households generally borrow money at either the standard variable rate (or SVR), which changes monthly with the Bank of England's official interest rate, or for a relatively short fixed period

How debt repayments change with official interest rates

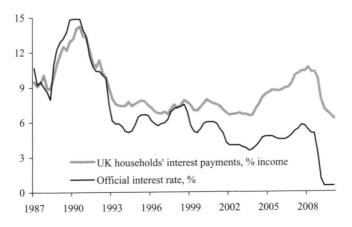

– usually two to five years. In the US and much of Europe, however, people tend to borrow for longer periods of time (above 10 years and often up to 25–30 years) at fixed interest rates. Thus, while monthly debt repayments for UK households typically change regularly, those in the US and Europe tend to be much more stable over time.

BORROWING BY FIRMS

When households borrow money it is usually done through the sort of financial intermediary that you would see on your local High Street. While specialist lenders do exist, by far the majority of loans are provided by banks and building societies.

When it comes to firms, however, the situation is a little different. For small and medium sized enterprises (or SMEs, as they are known), banks are typically the only source of funding. But when it comes to larger companies, bank funding is often not an option due to the sheer amount of money that needs to be raised. Rather, larger companies access the financial markets directly by issuing bonds and shares which are bought by investors. Some countries, such as the US, rely on so called capital market funding more than others.

A bond is nothing more than an IOU – a piece of paper that promises to pay the holder interest (known as the 'coupon') at regular intervals during the life of the loan. When the loan matures the company repays the initial loan provided by the investor. There are various types of bonds that companies can issue, typically categorised by how long the loan is for – or its 'maturity'. Firms' short term funding needs (usually for just a few months) are often satisfied by issuing what is called 'commercial paper', while corporate bonds are usually longer in maturity (years not months). The interest rate investors will require over and above the (usually) safer similar maturity bonds issued by the government will depend on the risk that the company defaults on its loan.

We can link all of this back to the amount of money in the economy. Remember from the start of the chapter that the broadest measures of money include not only the amount of cash we hold but also the money in our bank accounts and, in some cases, holdings of bonds. When governments and firms borrow money over short periods of time this can be classified as money supply. As we pointed out above – one person's debt is another person's monetary wealth.

THE EFFECT OF BORROWING ON THE ECONOMY

Just like changes in the amount of money in the economy, the amount of new borrowing being extended to households and firms is an important driver of economic growth. The chart below shows this – look how closely changes in borrowing influence the rate of economic growth in the US. There are actually few years over almost the past century where borrowing and activity have not moved together.

Sometimes, weaker demand in the economy naturally leads to fewer people borrowing money. But that's not always the case: sometimes things happen the other way round. A good example here is the credit crisis that started in 2007, where initially banks sharply reduced their lending to households and firms, which then led to a global recession. Given its importance and to conclude this chapter we'll now take a brief look at how the credit crisis came about and what lessons we can take for the future.

The relationship between US borrowing and activity

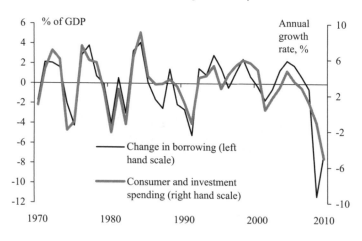

THE 2007 CREDIT CRISIS – IN A NUTSHELL

The credit crisis may have first hit the headlines over the summer of 2007, but it has its roots much earlier than that. The crisis began in the sub-prime market. Mortgage loans made to US households – who were least able to pay the money back when interest rates increased, house prices fell and unemployment rose – started to turn sour. This didn't only affect US banks, but banks and investors worldwide that those loans had been sold on to.

This happened through a process known as securitisation, whereby banks initially making the mortgage loan to households packaged up similar loans together and sold them on as job lots. The following graph shows how it all worked. This process helped the initiating banks to clear their books and lend even more money to the wrong type of household: those who too often had No Income, No Job or Assets (earning them the acronym NINJAs!).

The packaged loans were called 'collateralised debt obligations' – quite a mouthful, but helpfully abbreviated to CDOs. The problem was that no one knew how much exposure banks and investors globally had to these CDOs – with the result that they simply weren't willing to lend to one another for fear that they would fail under the weight of these unknown bad debts.

How securitisation works

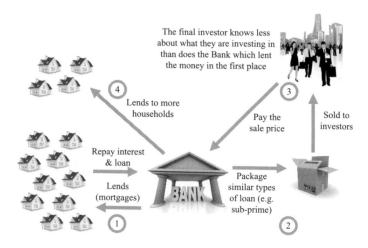

The final investor knows less about what they are investing in than does the Bank which lent the money in the first place

4 Lends to more households

3 Pay the sale price

Sold to investors

Repay interest & loan

Lends (mortgages)

1

Package similar types of loan (e.g. sub-prime)

2

Some banks did indeed fail, with Northern Rock in the UK and Lehman Brothers in the US two of the highest profile losers. RBS and Lloyds were in such dire straits that the British government ended up having to financially support them.

As we saw above, when banks aren't willing to lend the economy weakens. The scale of the recent credit crunch led not only to an economic downturn but to a global recession. This in turn placed great strain on governments whose spending had surged because of increased unemployment benefit payments, policy measures to kickstart the economy, and financial support for their ailing banking sectors.

WHO YOU NEED TO KNOW
Hyman P. Minsky

There has been something of a revival in interest in Hyman Minsky over the past few years, partly as a result of the recent credit crunch. In his 1986 book *Stabilising an Unstable Economy* he laid out the anatomy of credit crises (something he had been developing for many years previously), arguing that long periods of apparently benign economic stability can end up generating financial crises.

He identified three key types of borrower: those that were 'hedged', where the income they received from their investments was enough to meet the interest payments on their debt; those he called 'speculative' who have to keep borrowing to repay their debts; and finally 'Ponzi' borrowers (after Charles Ponzi, the American financial conman) who are only solvent because of rising asset prices.

As a period of economic stability continues, an increasing number of people fall into the latter

category as bubbles in asset prices (such as
shares and real estate) develop and debt rises
to ever higher levels. At some point, people
decide that enough is enough and try to sell
their assets, the result being that the bubble
bursts. The Ponzi investors are the first to default
on their loans as their investments were only
profitable as long as asset prices kept rising.
In response banks hold back from lending,
which in turn brings down the speculative
borrower – who, remember, was reliant on
bank finance. By the end of the process,
even the previously solvent hedged investor
can't get a loan, and the whole process
culminates in recession.

Minsky called this gradual move from a
stable economy to financial crisis the
Financial Instability Hypothesis. Since then,
the point at which investors try to get out at
the top has been nicknamed the 'Minsky Moment'.
He used his arguments to support the idea of
government intervention in the financial sector
and criticised the trend towards financial
deregulation in the 1980s.

Governments and central banks have learned a lot from this crisis. They have had to react quickly by pumping massive amounts of money (or 'liquidity') into the banking sector to keep it ticking, keeping interest rates at very low levels for a long time to offset the otherwise high borrowing costs that the credit crisis caused, and provide substantial rescue packages to their beleaguered financial sectors. The cost of the global rescue proved so high for governments that investors even began to doubt the solvency of some states – in some cases, such as Greece, their doubts were well founded.

If there's one thing we can take from the credit crisis it's this: money really does make the world go round, and when it dries up so too does economic activity. Over the coming years governments worldwide are changing the way that economic policy and banking regulation is conducted to prevent a repeat of the credit crisis.

WHAT YOU NEED TO READ

▶ For a history of money throughout the ages see Niall Ferguson, *The Ascent of Money*, Penguin, 2009.

▶ A generally good all round introductory economics text book – which has particularly accessible sections on money and monetary policy – is Michael Parkin, Melanie Powell, Kent Matthews, *Economics*, Addison Wesley, 2007.

▶ The Bank of England provides a clear discussion of money & credit (and more) in the Education section of its website, which can be found here: *www.bankofengland.co.uk/education/targettwopointzero/economy/money_financial_markets.htm.*

▶ A more detailed book which looks at some of the concepts in this chapter in more depth is by Keith Bank, *The Economics of Money, Banking and Finance: A European Text,* Financial Times/Prentice Hall, 2008.

▶ A very readable introduction to the credit crisis is Vince Cable, *The Storm.* Atlantic Books, 2010.

IF YOU ONLY REMEMBER ONE THING

Money is more than just the notes and coins we carry around in our pockets. The amount of money in the economy can significantly affect interest rates, activity and inflation. When it dries up, as in the credit crunch, the consequences for an economy can be dire.

WHAT IT'S ALL ABOUT

▶ What the role of central banks is in the economy

▶ How central banks change interest rates

▶ How interest rates affect the economy

▶ Why central banks target inflation

▶ What happens when interest rates get near zero

▶ How quantitative easing can boost the economy

WHAT DO CENTRAL BANKS DO?

Central banks are essentially the money managers of an economy. They are responsible for monetary policy. By this we mean they try to control the supply and value of money by issuing bank notes or setting interest rates. This is a vital role because as we saw in Chapter 5 money and credit form the very lifeblood of modern economies. If money and credit rise too quickly, businesses may not be able to keep up with the demands for increased production. As a result, they may raise prices which then causes inflation. In contrast, if the amount of money and credit are insufficient for the economy's needs, spending may fall and recession could follow.

The Bank of England in the UK, the Federal Reserve in the United States and the European Central Bank in the euro area all attempt to regulate the flow of money and credit by setting an interest rate – effectively the price of money – in order to control inflation and ensure their economies run smoothly.

For example, suppose the economy is growing too fast and the central bank becomes worried about rising inflation. It could then raise interest rates. This would make it costlier for businesses to borrow and it would raise household mortgage payments. In turn, demand in the economy would slow and inflationary pressures would ease.

If instead, the economy was in recession, the central bank could cut interest rates – making it cheaper to get money – in a bid to kick start demand by giving consumers a little bit extra in their pockets or encouraging companies to invest in new projects.

These days, most central banks in major developed economies tend to be independent. This means they are free from political control to set interest rates or manage the money supply. In the UK, the Bank of England was given 'operational independence' in 1997, meaning it has the power to set interest rates in order to achieve an inflation target set by the government.

The Bank of England has a 9-member Monetary Policy Committee that meets every month to decide what the right level of interest rates should be. They set rates in order to keep the CPI measure of inflation at 2%. That target is called symmetrical because undershooting it is considered just as bad as overshooting it – an inflation rate of 1% would be regarded as just as bad a miss as a rate of 3%.

The European Central Bank has a 22-member Governing Council which also meets monthly to set interest rates for the euro area and is charged with ensuring price stability which it defines as inflation at or just below 2%. The US Federal Reserve has a 12-member Federal Open Market Committee which meets eight times a year and has a dual mandate of price stability and sustainable economic growth. Of course, policymakers can always convene emergency meetings to change interest rates if the circumstances warrant it. A number of major central banks did just that after the September 11 attacks on the United States in 2001.

Financial markets remain very focused on central bank decisions because they affect the price of currencies, bonds and almost every other financial instrument. In that respect, the Federal Reserve or Fed as it is commonly called is perhaps the most important because of the giant size of the US economy and the US dollar's status as the world's most traded currency.

Pronouncements by central bankers are regarded with great reverence. Banks and financial institutions often employ armies of people to decipher their Delphic

WHO SAID IT

"Whoever controls the volume of money in any country is absolute master of all industry and commerce."
– James A. Garfield

utterances to get a better idea of what the central bank's next policy decision will be. Former Fed chairman Alan Greenspan became famous for never giving anything away. Some commentators even resorted to using the colour of his tie to guess what he was he was going to do on interest rates!

But setting interest rates is not a central bank's only function. They issue bank notes, manage payment systems and act as a bank for all the other banks in their economies. They are the backbone of the financial system, allowing banks to settle accounts with each other, businesses to receive payments and people to receive salaries. The total value of the UK payments system, for example, is more than £800 trillion annually. Central banks also often have responsibility for supervision of banks and other financial institutions.

HOW CENTRAL BANKING STARTED

The Bank of Amsterdam, set up in 1609, is often thought of as the forerunner to the modern-day central bank. Before then, most monetary transactions in Europe were conducted by the exchange of gold and silver coins. But the Bank of Amsterdam started allowing people to deposit their gold and silver with it in exchange for a small fee. The depositors would receive a credit in the bank's books, and this credit became known as bank money. A law was subsequently passed that all bills over

600 guilders had to be settled with bank money, creating a natural demand for accounts at the bank.

Probably the first example of a central bank as we know them now, however, was the establishment of the Bank of England in 1694. Affectionately nicknamed The Old Lady of Threadneedle Street, it was initially set up as the government of the day looked to borrow money from private investors to fund its war efforts, and acquired the responsibility to print money backed with gold.

In America, the First Bank of the United States came into being in 1791, modelled on the Bank of England. But strong political opposition meant its charter expired in 1811 and was not renewed. The Second Bank of the United States was set up in 1816 but that too suffered the same fate in 1836. Subsequent financial panics led to pressure for the creation of a strong central bank and the Federal Reserve was born in 1913. The European Central Bank, meanwhile, is the youngest of the major central banks as it was established in 1999 alongside the launch of the euro, Europe's single currency.

INTEREST RATES

Interest rates are the most powerful tool central banks have to meet their objectives of keeping inflation down or the economy on an even keel. They cut rates or 'loosen' monetary policy to stimulate the economy by making money cheaper. And they raise rates or 'tighten' monetary policy to cool the economy down and prevent inflation from picking up by raising the cost of borrowing.

The interest rates being talked about in this respect are usually very short term interest rates – the rates financial institutions charge each other for loans to be repaid over a very short period, for example, the next day. Central banks can either set the rate by lending and borrowing at that rate or by actively managing the money supply.

The Federal Reserve, for instance, will announce its target for the overnight interest rate which in the US is called the federal funds rate. It then increases or reduces the money supply to achieve that goal. It does this by buying and selling securities like bonds – transactions that are known as open market operations or OMOs.

So how does that work? Banks in the US, like in many other countries, are required by law to hold a minimum level of cash reserves with the central bank. This reserve requirement or cash reserve ratio as it is known is typically a percentage of the financial institution's demand accounts (deposits that can be withdrawn instantly and without penalty). The requirement is there to ensure that banks do not run out of cash when customers want to make withdrawals.

On any given day, a bank might make new loans which mean that its cash holdings dip below the reserve requirement. Under normal circumstances, it would then have to top up its reserves by borrowing the money from another bank which had excess reserves. The interest rate for the overnight transaction would be negotiated between the two banks and the weighted average of all such transactions is known as the federal funds effective rate.

Now suppose the Fed wants to reduce interest rates. It will do this by buying bonds from financial institutions. This will give the banks extra money as the Fed pays for its purchases with cash. As we have seen time and time again, what happens when the supply of something goes up? Its price comes down. And remember, the interest rate is just the price of money. So the rise in the money supply will push the interest rate or fed funds effective rate down toward the fed funds target.

If the Fed wanted to raise interest rates, it would sell bonds to banks. They would pay for those with cash, reducing the money supply and thus putting upward pressure on interest rates.

THE TRANSMISSION MECHANISM

But how do those central bank rates affect the economy? First of all, the overnight lending rates then become a benchmark for all the various interest rates in the economy.

A change in the main central bank rate or even a change in expectations of the main rate can set off a chain reaction which first affects other short-term interest rates, then longer-term interest rates, the value of the currency, stock prices and ultimately consumer and business spending decisions.

The full effect a change in interest rates has on the economy can take as long as two years and there are a variety of different channels through which it works. This process is called the transmission mechanism.

The change in the official interest rate has four main effects:

1. It influences all the other interest rates in the economy, like the one the banks pay into your savings account or you pay the bank on your mortgage.

The transmission mechanism – how interest rates affect the economy

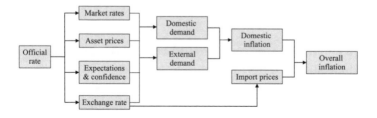

2. It can affect asset prices like the stock or housing market.
3. It can affect a country's exchange rate by making holding that currency more or less attractive.
4. It can alter expectations and confidence.

All of these effects can have a direct impact on demand in the economy. Let's take a look at each of these in turn. For a start, a cut in interest rates will encourage spending as it makes saving less attractive and borrowing more attractive. Lower rates should also cut financing costs for businesses and mortgage costs for consumers, giving them more money to spend. On the other hand, cutting interest rates will also reduce the amount of income savers get from their deposits. But borrowers tend to spend more of their money than lenders so in total interest rate cuts are expected to boost demand.

An interest rate cut can also have the effect of boosting stock prices or house prices partly because it becomes easier to finance borrowing. This then raises the wealth of the holders of those assets, encouraging more demand. Higher house prices might also encourage homeowners to extend their mortgages because they can borrow more on the higher value of their home, giving them more money to spend.

A cut in interest rates should reduce the value of the domestic currency. This should boost the sale of exports as these become cheaper to foreign buyers thereby stimulating the economy. At the same time, the fall in the value of the currency discourages the use of imports as it makes them more expensive, thereby encouraging the switch to domestically-produced goods.

Finally, confidence may also be boosted by a cut in interest rates, especially if the reduction builds expectations of more cuts to come. For example, in October 2008, many of the world's major central banks got together to cut interest rates on the same day in a bid to revive confidence following the collapse of the giant investment bank Lehman Brothers. Again the effect of a rise in confidence should be higher spending or aggregate demand than would otherwise have been the case.

Suppose then a central bank has cut interest rates and the effect is to boost spending through all the channels mentioned above. What happens next? How might this translate into higher inflation? Well, to begin with the increased demand in the economy should lead to higher output and jobs as producers try and keep pace with the extra spending power.

The supply and demand dynamics of the economy will change. Workers may ask for higher wages as they are now more in demand. The cost of raw materials may go up as producers' demand for them rises because they're making more goods. At the same time, the fall in the currency's value should boost the price of imported goods. Producers may have to pay more for their raw materials they buy from abroad, perhaps for important commodities like oil.

Producers will then try and recoup their higher costs through charging higher prices themselves and ultimately the price rises will move on to consumers, raising inflation. Conversely, a rise in interest rates would work the other way and have the effect of ultimately depressing inflation.

FORECASTING

Of course, none of this happens overnight or quite as simply in the real world. Monetary policy takes a long time to take effect and policymakers have to build this lag in the transmission mechanism into their decisions on interest rates. Economists reckon it can take as long as a year for the full effect of a change in interest rates to affect output or growth in the economy. It can take up to two years for the full effects to be felt on inflation.

The situation is further complicated because central bankers don't have access to perfect information on what is happening with prices or the economy at any given time. Economic data is often published with time lags and is subject to revision.

For example, in 1998, surveys suggested the global economy had slowed very sharply because of the emerging markets crisis we talked about in Chapter 4. Central banks cut interest rates as a result. Figures published much later showed the economy had actually been growing strongly just when policymakers had been most worried. The rate cuts then helped fuel the dotcom boom of 1999 and 2000 when stock prices of technology firms went through the roof.

Still, central bankers have to base their policy decisions on what information is available at the time and what that says about the outlook for the economy over the following two to three years.

To this end, they construct elaborate economic models which try and gauge what will happen to the economy over a few years and produce regular forecasts. Investors pay very close attention to those forecasts because it gives them an indication of where interest rates are probably headed.

The economist Robert Lucas argued in the 1970s that you couldn't just predict the future using the past as a reliable guide. His argument was that people will adjust their behaviour in response to policy being changed. According to the Lucas Critique, economists trying to predict the effect of a policy change should look at how it will affect individual actions and then aggregate those results across the economy. These models built up from the individual level or what we call the microfoundations are now the norm in central banking circles and are called dynamic stochastic general equilibrium (DSGE) models.

Even so, the predictions using these models remain just that, or best guesses. Many events will be outside the central bank's control. For example, there may be a change in government policy which changes the outlook for the economy. Alternatively, there could be a surge in commodity prices such as oil and gas which sends inflation up but slows growth as companies and consumers find themselves unable to pay the higher costs. There could be a natural disaster or a war.

Economists refer to such events as shocks and they can throw central bank forecasts out of kilter. For this reason, many central banks like to publish their forecasts as a range of probabilities. The chart below shows the percentage chance the Bank of England's two-year-ahead projections for inflation come within a percentage point of its 2% target. In August 2006, the central bank thought it had a more than 80% chance this would happen. It was less than half that four years later.

Likelihood (%) of inflation being within 1% of target in 2 years

INFLATION TARGETING

Ideas based around the work of the economist John Maynard Keynes dominated policymaking after the Second World War. Keynesianism advocated expansionary policies in a recession and contractionary policies during a boom. Suppose the economy was heading into a downturn. Governments could run up deficits and the central bank would cut interest rates. Alternatively, if inflation was picking up, governments could raise taxes or curb spending and the central bank could raise interest rates.

The success of these policies continued all the way into the 1960s and many economists thought they had found the Holy Grail to preserve prosperity. But the general consensus fell apart in the 1970s when huge rises in oil prices caused stagflation in many advanced economies. As we learned in Chapter 2, stagflation is when inflation is high and growth is weak. Expansionary policies were needed to boost the economy but contractionary policies were required to bring down inflation at exactly the same time.

The failure of Keynesianism to come up with a solution led to greater interest in other schools of economic thought and it was a philosophy known as monetarism that gained the most credence. Monetarists, led by the US economist Milton Friedman, argued that changes in the money supply would affect output in the short run and prices in the long run. Central banks, they argued, should therefore target the money supply.

Monetary targeting was widely used by central banks in the 1980s. In the United States, the Fed under the stewardship of Paul Volcker and the UK government of Margaret Thatcher successfully used targeting of the money supply to bring the very high rates of 1970s inflation down to more manageable levels. The European Central Bank had an explicit target for money supply growth when it was set up in 1999.

Monetary targets were called into question, however, in the late 1980s and 1990s when the relationship between the money supply and inflation appeared to break down. Many economists argued it would be better for central banks to target inflation itself. The goal for the central bank would be a particular rate of inflation and it would use policy (that is, interest rates) to try and ensure that rate.

New Zealand became the first country to adopt inflation targeting in 1990. Britain also announced the start of inflation targeting in 1992. Around 25–30 central banks now target inflation. The Fed, European Central Bank and Bank of Japan don't have explicit inflation targets but have adopted many of the elements of an inflation targeting regime.

Inflation targeting frameworks tend to have four main features:

1. An explicit central bank commitment to maintain low and stable inflation as the main goal of monetary policy.

2. An actual numerical target or range for inflation.

Countries with inflation targeting regimes

Country	Date started
New Zealand	1990
Canada	1991
United Kingdom	1992
Sweden	1993
Australia	1993
Czech Republic	1997
Israel	1997
Poland	1998
Brazil	1999
Chile	1999
Colombia	1999
South Africa	2000
Thailand	2000
Korea	2001
Mexico	2001
Iceland	2001
Norway	2001
Hungary	2001
Peru	2002
Philippines	2002
Guatemala	2005
Indonesia	2005
Romania	2005
Turkey	2006
Serbia	2006
Ghana	2007

3. Accountability, ensuring policymakers are visibly taken to task for missing their target.
4. A forward-looking approach to targeting inflation.

Targets tend to be set at around 2% to build in some margin of error against falling into deflation which is generally considered to be more problematic and harder to get out of than inflation.

Proponents of inflation targeting say the system ensures greater confidence in public policymaking and removes a bias for inflationary policies. Investors can be confident that the central bank will act to keep inflation low. Critics argue that it can lead to policymakers being too focused on inflation at a risk of ignoring other things going on in the economy, such as the formation of asset bubbles or unemployment.

MONETARY POLICY RULES

Some central bankers would argue that monetary policy is an art and not a science. A number of economists, however, have argued it is better to have rules which prescribe what action to take depending on the state of the economy at the time.

One such rule is the Taylor Rule after the economist and former US Treasury official John Taylor. The idea is that

WHO YOU NEED TO KNOW
Robert Barro

Robert Barro is a US economist based at Harvard University. Initially a physics graduate from the California Institute of Technology, Barro turned to economics and got his PhD from Harvard in 1970. Considered one of the most influential modern-day economists, his 1984 textbook *Macroeconomics* is widely used in college courses.

Barro's work has been pivotal in the adoption of explicit inflation targets for central banks. Together with David Gordon, he put forward the theory of inflation being a 'dynamic inconsistency' problem. Think of it as a game played between the central bank and the public. According to their argument, central banks will often be tempted into breaking their own inflation targets in order to raise employment. As a result, the public will deduce the target won't be met and raise their own inflation expectations. The end result will be higher inflation and the target will be missed.

That is why, the theory goes, central banks should have explicit inflation targets which they are required to achieve to ensure there is public confidence in their ability and desire to keep inflation down. It explains why the accountability feature of inflation targeting is so important.

Barro has also been a big proponent of rational expectations theory. This is a branch of economics which holds that individuals, or economic agents as they are called, act rationally to maximise their self-interest. In 1974, he wrote a very influential paper called *"Are government bonds net wealth?"* which argued that tax cuts now would have little effect as rational individuals would realise that they would have to be paid for in the future through higher taxes and so would not adjust their present spending patterns. This concept, known as Ricardian Equivalence after the nineteenth century English economist David Ricardo, is still actively debated now.

if inflation is picking up or the economy was running too fast, this rule would prescribe how much interest rates need to be raised by to bring it under control. If the economy was weakening, the rule would say how far interest rates should be brought down.

The formula for devising the actual amounts by which interest rates should be raised or lowered would be based on looking at a period in which monetary policy was considered to have done a good job in managing the economy and inflation.

Arguments for central banks adopting such rules include that it would allow policymakers to communicate their actions better. Also, if policy is based on a well-established rule, then the central bank's accountability and credibility may increase. Financial markets will also find it easier to forecast future policy decisions and this will reduce uncertainty, which is good for investment decisions.

But there are also arguments against. One is that the right level of interest rates compatible with longer term goals might vary over time. There is also a lot of uncertainty around where precisely the economy is in relation to full employment – a key input into a monetary policy rule.

While there remains considerable debate about the use of rules, most major central banks like the Fed, Bank of England and European Central Bank still don't subscribe to any pre-set stipulations and favour what is known as 'constrained discretion'.

WHO YOU NEED TO KNOW
John Taylor

Born in 1946, Stanford University professor John Taylor has been at the forefront of economic policymaking and theory since the 1970s. He studied first at Princeton University before getting his PhD at Stanford.

Between 2001 and 2005, Taylor was the US Treasury's Under Secretary for International Affairs where he was responsible for policies on currencies, international debt and oversight of the International Monetary Fund. He was also a member of the President's Council of Economic Advisers from 1989 to 1991.

He is most famous for his formulation of the Taylor Rule in 1992 which suggested that the Federal Reserve could set interest rates using a simple equation looking at the current rate of inflation and where the economy was in relation to its trend level of output. According to Taylor, the equation also explained what the Fed had been doing over the past five years.

The rule caused an immediate stir in both financial markets and among policymakers. Soon, Fed staff were providing the central bank's rate-setting committee with various permutations of the rule before each interest rate decision. Taylor was even invited into the Fed to discuss the rule and its application with Fed policymakers in 1995.

But Alan Greenspan, chairman of the Fed through the 1990s, believed that discretion was better than a rules-based approach to setting interest rates. The Taylor Rule, he said, only worked if the future was like the past. 'Unfortunately, however, history is not an infallible guide to the future,' Greenspan argued.

QUANTITATIVE EASING

In this chapter we have seen that central banks can cut interest rates to try and stimulate an economy when it is slowing down and facing the threat of recession. They can also raise interest rates to slow an economy down to prevent inflation. But while interest rates can keep going up if need be, there is clearly a lower limit for them – zero. That is why it can be much easier to stop an economic boom than pull out of a deep bust.

The economist John Maynard Keynes summarised this problem by describing trying to get an economy out of a severe recession as 'like pushing on a string.' Another way of putting it is that it's easy to curb demand but harder to create it when it doesn't exist. The economy is said to be in a liquidity trap when monetary policy is no longer effective at stimulating demand. This might be because people prefer to hold on to cash no matter how much the supply of money increases or interest rates fall, perhaps because they expect prices to fall further meaning they'd be better off postponing any spending.

So what happens when interest rates are already at zero or close to it and the economy still needs more support? This is the situation policymakers in Japan found themselves in during the early 2000s. The Japanese economy had slowed sharply after the collapse of its bubble economy in the late 1980s/early 1990s. By 1995, it was experiencing deflation. Successive huge government spending programmes and interest rates being held at close to zero appeared to have no effect at lifting the economy out of its depression.

Then in March 2001, the Bank of Japan, the country's central bank, embarked on its now-famous policy of quantitative easing. Instead of just setting the interest rate at zero, the central bank flooded the market with new money by buying securities like long-term Japanese government bonds from banks.

WHO SAID IT

"The US government has a technology, called a printing press (or, today, its electronic equivalent), that allows it to produce as many US dollars as it wishes at essentially no cost."
– **Ben Bernanke**

In effect, the Bank of Japan was creating new money and putting it into the banking system. That is why quantitative easing, or QE, is often popularly referred to as a policy of printing money. Of course, there are no actual banknotes being printed. Banks' accounts with the central bank are just credited with the extra funds, just in the same way as if your bank credited your account, except in this case the central bank would have created the money out of thin air.

The Bank of England also started its own quantitative easing programme in March 2009 after first cutting interest rates to a record low of 0.5% in the depths of the 2008/09 recession. It too created new money and bought with it mostly UK government bonds from banks in the hope that they would start lending the cash and boost spending in the economy.

How does this actually work? The central bank simply offers to buy several billion pounds of bonds from financial institutions on a regular basis. Participating banks would sell the bonds and in return saw their accounts at the central bank credited with the cash.

How quantitative easing works

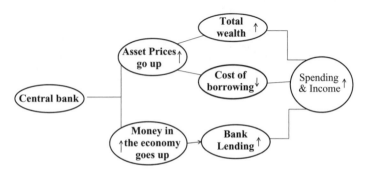

The idea is that the financial institutions can use the extra cash to spend on goods or services or other assets. Asset prices should also increase, making people feel richer. At the same time, banks should be willing to lend more as their money holdings have increased and the cost of borrowing should fall. The improvement in credit conditions and rise in wealth should then encourage people and businesses to spend more, boosting the overall economy.

While quantitative easing at its simplest aims to boost the money supply to stimulate spending, central banks can also target which securities they buy with the newly-created money to affect their prices and change overall credit conditions in the economy. For example, the Fed conducted its own version of quantitative easing in 2009 which it preferred to call credit easing. In this, it bought mortgage-backed securities – pools of mortgage loans – in a bid to reduce the cost of home loans and make them more available. The Feb went on to expand its quantitative easing programme to government bonds in 2010.

But the real question for quantitative easing is whether it works. Economists remain divided on this. Japan continued with its policy of quantitative easing until 2006 and while the economy did begin to grow in this period, the recovery was never spectacular. Some argue that things would have been even worse for Japan without the extra money pumped into the economy and others say it made no difference at all. Similarly, policymakers in the US and UK argue their programmes stopped a bad situation getting worse and did help the economy by bringing down borrowing costs for companies and consumers.

Critics of quantitative easing argue that it could lead to hyperinflation, the phenomenon of sharply rising prices discussed in Chapter 2, because of all the excess money being put into the economy. An opposite problem is if banks hoard the extra cash in order to rebuild their own balance sheets that might have been showing hefty losses. The result would be that the extra money doesn't get into the economy.

FINANCIAL STABILITY

The role of central banks doesn't stop at managing demand and inflation in the economy. They typically have an important role in maintaining financial stability. By this, we mean that they watch over the health of the entire financial system. They oversee how banks do business and ensure that markets are running smoothly.

They also often fulfil a function that is known as being the lender of last resort. This is an institution that is willing to extend credit when no one else will. So a bank unable to borrow elsewhere could go to a central bank as a last-ditch effort to raise funds. Usually, the central bank as the lender of last resort would provide the money needed but at a much higher interest rate than it would normally charge.

Usually, few institutions avail themselves of such a facility because of the stigma of it becoming known they were unable to get credit anywhere else. This could in fact exacerbate their bad credit standing and put further pressure on them.

This is what happened to the Northern Rock bank in the UK in 2007. Unable to raise any more money, the bank was forced to call on the Bank of England's emergency lending facility to help tide it over. When news that Northern Rock was using the facility broke, there was a stampede of depositors trying to get their money out as they feared the bank was about to go bust – the first bank run in the UK in nearly 150 years.

Central banks might also be reluctant to always stand ready to provide funding for any bank that needs it. That is because knowing the central bank was always available with more funds might encourage banks to take excessive risk. Economists call this the problem of moral hazard. Insurance companies, for example, try deal with this all the time by having an 'excess.' Policyholders have to absorb that cost themselves before they receive any payout so as to ensure they take some care themselves.

Still, central banks have to stand ready to provide emergency funding because they may also be worried that the collapse of one bank could have consequences for many others and the financial system as a whole. This is known as systemic risk. The collapse of the investment bank Lehman Brothers in 2008 generated a lot of debate among regulators about whether some banks are too big to fail. By this, they mean banks that are so large that their collapse could endanger the whole financial system because of the interconnected nature of markets.

Since then, there has also been a lot more focus on central banks taking what is called a macro-prudential approach. This means they should look at the effect of any regulatory policies not just on an individual bank, but on the banking system as a whole. The thinking is that while it may be okay for one bank to have borrowed a certain amount, it would be really bad if every bank was equally in debt. Central banks, some economists argue, should be given powers to manage this type of risk if there is to be a safer financial system.

These could include controls over how much banks lend to prevent excessive speculation. For example, one idea many economists talk about is giving central banks a say over how big a mortgage anyone gets. The central bank might be able to set a limit on banks lending anything more than, say, three times someone's salary for a home loan.

The central banks of the future will likely not just have powers over setting interest rates but may have a whole arsenal of new weapons to maintain financial stability and keep the economy ticking.

WHAT YOU NEED TO READ

▶ The Federal Reserve has an excellent website explaining the history of the US central bank and how it works. *www.federalreserve.gov/*.

▶ The Bank for International Settlements is the bank for central banks and its website has a useful collection of articles and discussions about all the latest issues. *www.bis.org/*.

▶ For a detailed look at the benefits of inflation targeting, consider reading *Inflation Targeting: Lessons from the International Experience* by Ben Bernanke, Thomas Laubach, Frederic Mishkin & Adam Posen, Princeton University Press, 1999.

▶ For a riveting account of the 2008/09 crisis and the Fed's response, have a look at *In Fed We Trust* by David Wessel, Random House, 2009.

▶ For the problems faced by Japan's policy-makers in trying to get their economy out of deflation, have a look at *Japan's Policy Trap* by Akio Mikuni and R. Taggart Murphy, Brookings Institution Press, 2002.

IF YOU ONLY REMEMBER ONE THING

Central banks are the money managers of economies and are responsible for monetary policy. They can raise interest rates to slow the economy and keep inflation down and they can cut interest rates to boost demand in the economy.

CHAPTER 7

THE PUBLIC FINANCES

WHAT IT'S ALL ABOUT

- ▶ What the public finances are and their role in the economy
- ▶ Where the government gets it money from
- ▶ How government spending can help manage the economy
- ▶ What the budget deficit and national debt are
- ▶ How governments finance the deficit
- ▶ What the role of rating agencies is

WHAT ARE THE PUBLIC FINANCES?

Governments clearly have a big role to play in any economy, though the exact scale of their involvement can vary hugely across the world. They collect taxes. They build roads. They fund the police force and the army. They sometimes offer free healthcare and education. They typically pay benefits to the unemployed or the sick and elderly. Study of the public finances basically looks at all the ways in which governments bring in money and then spend it. These actions are collectively known as fiscal policy and in this chapter we will look at how that works and what effect it can have on an economy.

Up until the seventeenth century, governments would typically fund extra expenditure – wars were the greatest call on the public purse in those days – by levying new taxes. But by the late 1600s, governments had worked out they could also borrow money. They would have to pay interest but it gave them ready cash. And so the concept of a budget deficit was born and it continues to this day.

If revenues equal expenditure, the budget is in balance. But if spending outstrips the money coming in, the budget is in deficit. If revenues exceed expenditure, the budget is in surplus. Think about your own personal finances. If your take-home pay in one year is £50,000 but you spend £60,000, you'll need to borrow £10,000 to finance the extra expenditure – that's your deficit.

Alternatively, you might have only spent £40,000. In that case, you save £10,000 or are in surplus by that amount.

Most countries publish a monthly measure of their finances which records the size of all tax revenues minus government expenditure and any interest that has to be paid on existing debt. Totting up each month's deficit or surplus gives the budget balance for the year.

One common mistake is to confuse the deficit and the debt. The national debt as it is often called is the sum complete of surpluses and deficits over a long period of time and represents a country's complete obligations. So every year that a country runs a deficit, it adds to the national debt by that amount. Budget surpluses, however, can be used to pay down the debt.

While both the overall debt and annual budget balances are often expressed as cash figures, it may be better to look at them as a percentage of GDP. That is, as a proportion of the total economic output of the country. This makes both historical and international comparisons easier as obviously the bigger the economy, the bigger the deficit or debt might be in cash terms.

BALANCING THE BUDGET

So where does all the money go and where does it come from? Well, the revenue comes from mainly taxes. All the money you pay in income tax goes straight to the receipts side of the government finances. So does sales tax or the duty on a pack of cigarettes or a bottle of wine. Companies also have to pay corporation tax and there are all sorts of levies on various industries or transactions whether it's a tax on gambling or duty on fuel.

Spending, meanwhile, includes all the money the government has to shell out to keep services like hospitals and schools running. In the UK, for example, spending on the National Health Service (NHS) typically consumes close to 20% of total spending. Spending on social security is just under 30%.

Statisticians also like to differentiate between current and capital spending. The first is the spending that goes into welfare payments or salaries of public sector

The percentage breakdown of UK government spending

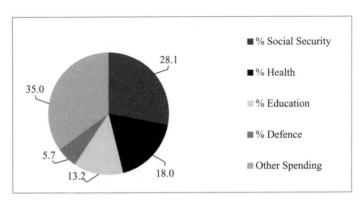

employees – the running costs of the country, if you like. The second is spending on infrastructure like new hospitals or roads – in other words, big one-off investments. Sometimes, economists talk about the primary balance. This is the budget balance excluding the cost of interest payments on existing debt.

Just like it makes sense to save up in good times so you have something tucked away for a rainy day, many economists advocate trying to balance a government's budget over the ups and downs of an economic cycle. There is no set timeframe for a cycle but think of it as a number of years which captures big variations in the speed at which economic output expands.

When the economy is growing fast, government revenues tend to go up because more people are in work, earning more money and thus paying more taxes. At the same time, the government probably has to pay less on unemployment benefits. Hence, it should be easier for governments to run a surplus.

But when the economy is slowing, government revenues tend to fall because people lose their jobs or companies make lower profits. Government spending, meanwhile, may increase because of higher benefit payments. The result: it's easier to notch up a deficit.

Simple economics, therefore, suggests that governments should run up surpluses in the good times which can then be run down by deficits in the bad times.

This allows for variations in the budget over time. Let's look at an example closer to home to illustrate these concepts. Suppose you paid your home heating bill by the same monthly direct debit amount each month. In summer months, you may be paying too much, or running up a surplus on your account. But in winter months, you may be paying too little, running up a deficit. Over the whole year, however, your total monthly payments should be sufficient to cover your annual bill.

Just as you would expect to use more gas in winter and less in summer, budget surpluses or deficits are considered to be natural byproducts of the economy moving up and down a gear. Tax receipts will be high and the need for social security spending low when the economy is doing well and the reverse when the economy is doing poorly. These natural changes in the tax take and spending as the economy goes up and down are referred to as the automatic stabilisers.

The deficit or surplus that occurs as a result of the ups and downs of the economy is called the cyclical balance. Going back to our example of a home heating bill, the shortfall between what you pay for in winter and what you have actually used could be thought of as a cyclical deficit. It would then be made up by a cyclical surplus in the summer months.

But say your total monthly payments still leave you paying for less gas than you have actually consumed over the year, you would then be still left with a shortfall or deficit in what you owe that would have to be paid at some stage.

In the same way, the government could have a shortfall where the deficit in a recession is not paid off when the economy is booming. This would be an example of a structural budget deficit.

How the budget balance is made up

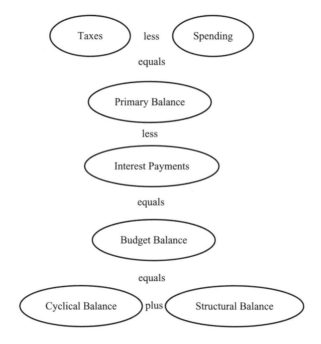

Just as you would then need to raise your monthly payments for a home heating bill, so the government would need either to change its spending plans or raise taxes to reduce the structural budget deficit.

Such explicit policy changes are known as discretionary fiscal policy in contrast to the non-discretionary or automatic changes which result from the business cycle. For example, if the government had a structural surplus, it could cut VAT. Or if it was judged that the structural budget deficit was too high, a government could start cutting spending by, for example, reducing the size of the army or civil servants.

While having a balanced budget over the economic cycle may be considered desirable, a big problem for economists is we can never be sure exactly where we are in the cycle. It can often take years before a full picture of where the economy is in the cycle emerges.

As a result, some economists have suggested the distinction between structural and cyclical budget balances is not that useful and have put forward the notion of a fiscal gap. This looks at the difference between spending and receipts over a long period of time and tries to account for future commitments and revenue streams.

For example, better living standards and healthcare mean many developed economies have an increasing number of elderly people in the population claiming state benefits like pensions. At the same time, there is a smaller proportion of younger people in jobs and paying taxes. This higher dependency ratio will result in bigger budget deficits or gaps in future years as there will be less money coming in and more money going out.

The UK's debt as a percentage of GDP

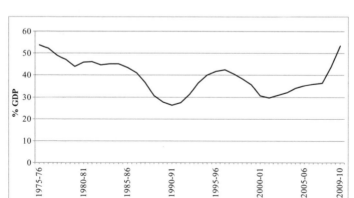

So economists calculating the fiscal gap would look at the deficit right now but also include an estimate for how much spending is likely to exceed revenues in the future because of the change in population trends.

THE ROLE OF GOVERNMENT

So government spending tends to rise and tax revenues tend to fall automatically in economic downturns and the reverse is true in the upswing just by nature of the business cycle – effects, as you will remember, we call the automatic stabilizers. But it is governments that decide tax rates and make spending decisions – what is known as discretionary fiscal policy.

What role the state should play in the economy is the subject of much debate and positions often divide along political lines. One view common in many advanced economies is the doctrine of *laissez-faire*, literally French for 'let do' or rather leave them to it. According to this view, governments should interfere little and let the private sector drive growth.

On the opposite side of the spectrum are those who call for a more interventionalist approach. They argue that the government should have the dominant role, controlling major industries and providing services. The truth is most developed economies are somewhere between these two extremes.

Most people agree the state has a clear role in providing what are called public and merit goods. Public goods have two key characteristics: they are non-excludable – you can't stop people using them; and they are non-rivalrous – one person using them does not diminish their use by another. Street lighting is a classic example because you can't exclude people from benefiting from it and one person going under the light doesn't make it any less bright.

In addition, there are also merit goods. Healthcare is a good example. It can and is provided privately. But there may not be enough health provision for everyone who needs it under a purely private system. It may be considered desirable, therefore, for people to have access to basic or even more advanced healthcare, which is where the state can step in.

Government spending as a percentage of national income in G7 countries

	2000	2010
France	51.6	55.9
UK	36.6	52.5
Italy	46.1	51.6
Germany	45.1	47.9
Canada	42.0	43.2
United States	33.9	41.6
Japan	39.0	40.8

You can see from the chart above just how much government spending in the UK rose as a proportion of GDP, from well below 40% in 2000 to above 50% by 2010. This reflects the choices that governments have over how much to tax and spend in an economy – in other words, how much of a role that the state plays in every day life.

THE KEYNESIAN APPROACH

The twentieth century economist John Maynard Keynes also advocated an active role for government to help smooth out the peaks and troughs of the economic cycle.

But how can government action actually do that? Well, fiscal policy can be used both directly and indirectly to affect demand. Spending decisions affect the economy directly and taxes indirectly.

First of all, imagine that an economy is in recession and demand is weak. A government can choose to expand fiscal policy – in others words, cut taxes or increase spending. Cutting taxes would put more money in people's pockets and so they would be able to go out and spend more, thereby providing an indirect boost to aggregate demand. Tax rises would do the reverse and could be used to dampen demand.

State spending, on the other hand, can have a direct effect on the economy as the extra money buys goods & services there was no demand for before. But according to Keynesian economists, the effect of extra government spending or tax cuts does not just end there. It has a knock-on effect which boosts the economy further.

Suppose the government cuts taxes and every family were to get an extra £50 each month which it then spends. The owners of the stores where they spend their windfall make more money and in turn they order more goods from factory owners who make more money themselves. This concept is referred to as the fiscal multiplier.

So if the government increases spending by a total of £1 billion but the knock-on effects from higher expenditure lead to overall GDP rising by £2 billion, then we say the multiplier is 2.

Keynes' views gained particular momentum after the Second World War when the massive military effort and forced reconstruction provided a sizable boost to the world economy. It was the mainstream economic view for much of the 1950s and 1960s with most governments accepting that they should try solve problems in the short run rather than let market forces handle them in the long run. But Keynes did not advocate loose fiscal policy all the time. Policy should only be loose to counter downturns. He also believed contractionary policy was needed when the economy was booming to quell inflation.

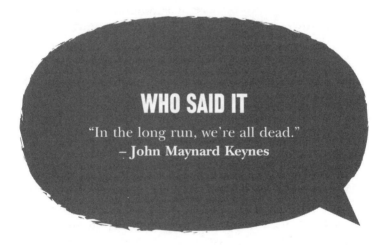

WHO SAID IT

"In the long run, we're all dead."
– **John Maynard Keynes**

Keynesian thinking came under fire in the 1970s with many economists questioning whether fiscal policy could have such a big impact because the extra spending had to be paid for at some stage. One argument against the use of fiscal policy to prop up demand is that people will just think they will have to pay for it in later years. According to this view, tax cuts will not fuel greater consumption because people understand they will push up the deficit which will then require tax rises in the future.

This concept is referred to as Ricardian Equivalence after the nineteenth century economist David Ricardo. It was later elaborated on by the economist Robert Barro in the 1970s.

The theory depends on several assumptions which many economists question. The first is that it assumes people make rational decisions about the future. Critics of this theory question whether people really think of tax cuts now in terms of tax rises later – surely they will just spend the money? The theory also assumes that people behave as if they're going to live forever. Many people might not care that higher deficits now will mean a higher tax burden for future generations.

Many economists argue that too much government spending can actually harm the economy because it stops the private sector from operating at its full potential. This is a concept that is known as crowding out. According to the theory, higher borrowing pushes up interest rates. This makes it more expensive for private businesses to invest and so curtails their growth. Some people also talk about crowding out when they see the state providing goods or services that otherwise could be provided by business. The assumption, of course, is that the private sector would provide these goods or services more efficiently.

WHO YOU NEED TO KNOW
Richard F. Kahn

Born in London to a German father, Kahn
studied under Keynes at Cambridge University
where he became a Fellow of Kings College
in 1930. He went on to become a professor
in 1951. He also worked for one of the leading
figures who opposed the Keynesian interventionist
approach becoming too distilled by those who
saw markets balancing themselves. He also
worked at times for the British Government
and the United Nations.

Kahn is known for developing the concept of
the multiplier in 1931 which then dominated
Keynesian thinking. According to Kahn's
employment multiplier, government action to
raise public sector employment by 100 jobs
would actually raise employment by a multiple
of that. This is because thee newly employed
people in the public sector would spend
more money, buying more goods which
would require more production, and thus
more jobs.

Keynes later used this notion for his own multiplier which shows total output in the economy rising by a multiple of a set increase in government spending.

He believed the multiplier for the US economy in the 1930s was as great as 2.5. That is to say for every dollar spent by the government, there would be $2.50 boost to the economy. So he argued the best way out of the Great Depression was for the government to raise borrowing and go on a spending spree.

Economists Carmen Reinhart and Kenneth Rogoff have suggested that countries with big public debts relative to the size of economic output tend to grow more slowly. The two economists argue that for advanced economic countries, those with public debt above 90% of GDP could have annual growth two percentage points lower than those with debt below 30% of GDP.

TAXES

We've already said that the main way the government earns money is through taxation. But how does it go about deciding what to tax and by how much? Again, this is a subject of much debate and principles can vary around the world depending on politics. Traditionally, more right-wing politicians argue for much lower taxes while the more left of centre prefer a system which is more redistributive to spread wealth in a society around.

The Scottish economist Adam Smith proposed four 'canons' or principles of taxation which most economists still hold to be true today. First of all, the cost of collection must be low relative to the amount being collected. Second, the timing and the amount to be paid should be certain to the payer. Third, the means and timing of payment should be convenient to the payer. Finally, taxes should be levied depending on the ability to pay.

Nowadays, economists also add another three principles. Any tax should involve the least loss of efficiency – that is it should not change people's behaviour. It should also be compatible with foreign tax systems and it should automatically adjust to changes in inflation.

The main types of taxation include: income tax, which applies to a person's earnings; corporation tax, which applies to a company's profits; VAT or sales tax which is levied on purchases; wealth tax, which can be exercised on a person's asset holdings – property is an example; and excise duty, which is an additional sales tax on items like cigarettes, alcohol or fuel.

In addition, economists distinguish between direct and indirect taxes. Income tax falls into the first category because it is applied to your own earnings and paid directly to the government. VAT on the other hand is an indirect tax because it is charged on goods or services that you pay to the vendor who then pays it to the government.

Economists also like to distinguish between progressive, regressive and proportional taxes. A progressive tax is one which the proportion paid increases as the amount being taxed goes up. This is common of most income tax systems in developed countries where people on higher incomes pay higher rates of tax. Typically, income tax involves a tax-free threshold under which the individual pays nothing. Anything above that then might be taxed at a basic rate, say 20%. Earnings above a particular level after that then might be taxed at an even higher rate, say 40%. This would mean those on higher income pay proportionately more and is in keeping with a view to the tax system being used to redistribute wealth.

A proportional tax is one where the percentage paid in taxation stays the same as income increases. This is often referred to as a flat tax as everyone, whatever their income, would pay the same rate of tax. A number of eastern European economies like Estonia and Lithuania have a flat tax regime.

Regressive taxes, on the other hand, are where the percentage paid in tax decreases as income increases. Common examples would be VAT or excise duties which are applied to the goods being taxed. While the rate as a percentage of the price of a good or service may be the same for everyone, it will take up a bigger slice of poorer people's incomes.

WHO SAID IT

"In this world nothing can be certain, except death and taxes."
– Benjamin Franklin

Economists also want tax systems to take account of inflation. So ideally they would want thresholds to rise in line with price rises in the economy. Governments also need to think about what the right level of taxation is because in some cases setting rates too high might actually be self-defeating. For example, many people still travel to continental Europe from Britain for so-called 'booze cruises' to stock up on alcohol to benefit from lower taxes in France. The UK government has to balance any decision to raise duty on alcohol at home against how many more people might start buying their drinks abroad.

Similarly, raising income or corporation tax too far might lead to people or businesses relocating abroad, or it could encourage people to find ways to escape tax altogether through loopholes and avoidance measures. Taxes that are too high may also discourage people from working more and instead opt to do nothing.

The Laffer curve, named after the US economist Arthur Laffer, tries to show what the relationship between government revenue and tax rates might look like. Laffer noted that if there were no taxes at all – that is the tax rate was zero – then the government would get no tax revenue. But if the tax rate was 100% – that is the government took everything you earned – then there would also be no tax revenue as there would be no reason for anyone to work (everything they earned would go in tax).

Therefore, he said that if you plotted a graph of tax revenue against tax rates, you would get a curve which showed that both zero and 100% tax rates produced no revenue. As tax rates rose above zero, so too did government revenue but at some point tax revenues would decline as the rate neared 100%.

The Laffer curve

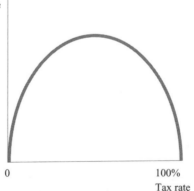

Tax Revenue

0   100%
Tax rate

WHO YOU NEED TO KNOW
Paul Samuelson

Paul Samuelson was a US economist who more than anyone popularised Keynesian economics around the world through his hugely influential textbook *Economics – An Introductory Analysis.* First published in 1948, the book has notched up 19 editions and sold more than four million copies, making it the biggest-selling economics textbook of all time.

He won the Nobel Prize for economics in 1970 and is credited with being the founder of what is known as the neo-classical synthesis – the marriage of interventionist Keynesian economics with the neo-classical tradition of individuals acting in their own interest. This combination of schools forms the bedrock of modern mainstream economic thinking.

His book, *Foundations of Economic Analysis,* argued that agents or participants in the economy try to get the best out of any situation whether by maximising their happiness or their profits.

He is also credited with coming up with the concept of comparative statics – which allows us to measure how changing something like tax rates can affect the whole economy.

Samuelson started his studies at the University of Chicago during the Great Depression and went on to Harvard before becoming a professor at the Massachusetts Institute of Technology, which he helped turn into a world-class school boasting several Nobel Prize winners. He also advised Presidents John F. Kennedy and Lyndon B. Johnson. His nephew Larry Summers is also a famous economist and former US Treasury Secretary.

234

While there is little empirical evidence to show just what that rate might be, the Laffer curve has been used widely by free-market economists to justify tax cuts when rates are high.

DEBT AND BOND MARKETS

So we've established the budget deficit is how much the government overspends versus the amount of revenue it collects from taxes. But where does this extra money come from? The answer to that for most modern economies is from the bond markets.

As we learnt in Chapter 5, bonds are essentially IOUs from governments or companies that issue them. Government bonds issued by the United States are known as US Treasuries and make up the largest bond market in the world. In the UK, they're called gilt-edged securities or gilts. In Germany, they're called bunds and Japanese government bonds are referred to as JGBs.

A government sells or issues bonds to raise money in international financial markets. For this, it pays a fixed rate of interest. This is why they are also known as fixed-income securities. The timeframe over which the initial value of the bond is paid back is known as its maturity. For example a government can issue a billion pounds worth of five-year bonds where at the end of that period it would have to pay the full billion pounds back as well as any interest along the way.

The interest rate that the government has to pay depends on the prevailing interest rate at the time, inflation and the perceived creditworthiness of the borrower government. So if a country were deemed to be less likely to be able to pay back their debt in future, investors would demand a higher interest rate to compensate them for the risk. The interest rate is known as the coupon of the bond. This is because bonds were historically issued as bearer certificates and several coupons were printed on them. The bearer of the bond would clip a coupon each time an interest payment was due and present it to the issuer government in exchange for cash.

Suppose that the coupon or interest rate on the £1 billion of five-year bonds is 3%. What this means is that the government would pay interest of 3% every year on the 1 billion pounds of bonds issued plus it would pay back the full amount at the end of five years. Alternatively, you can think of it like the investor or the buyer of the bond will get a 3% return every year on the face value of the bond and then get the entire principal back at the end of five years.

Bonds can have all sorts of maturities from a matter of a few days to 50 years or more. If they are to be paid back within a year, they are usually referred to as bills. The longer the maturity the higher the interest rate is likely to be as it means higher risk for investors who have to be compensated for locking their funds up for longer. The higher the interest rate, the more expensive it is for the government to finance its debt.

Economists and bond market practitioners often talk about the yield curve. This shows the relationship between the interest rate and the maturity of the bond. As you can see from the diagram below, a normal yield curve is upward-sloping as borrowers are likely to extract higher interest rates for longer-dated debt.

Sometimes, however, you might see a yield curve that is inverted or downward-sloping. In this scenario, bonds with shorter maturities will attract a higher interest rate. The UK has witnessed this phenomenon in the past

The shape of the yield curve

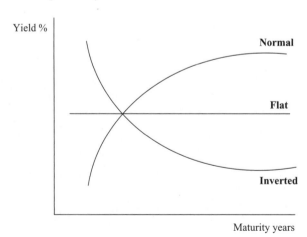

Yield %

Normal

Flat

Inverted

Maturity years

because of heavy pension fund demand for longer-dated bonds. But it could also occur because investors expect an economic slowdown which will lead to falling interest rates in the future. Highly inverted yield curves could be a signal the market expects a depression.

A flat yield curve is exactly that – there is little difference in the interest rates at varying maturities and this may happen in the transition period between normal and inverted yield curves.

Governments need to keep paying interest on their debt. If financial markets get a whiff that some country will not be able to meet its obligations of interest payments or redemptions (the repayment of the loan), then that state will likely see the interest rates it has to pay to finance or refinance its debt rise.

WHO SAID IT?

"I used to think that if there was reincarnation, I wanted to come back as the president or the pope or as a .400 baseball hitter. But now I would like to come back as the bond market. You can intimidate everybody."
– James Carville

Many economists argue that paying interest is essentially a waste of resources and that if borrowing becomes too high then more and more of a government's budget will be swallowed up by the costs of financing the debt alone, rather than being spent on goods & services. Another argument against running up too much debt is that it imposes a burden on future generations.

Investors can judge how safe any government bonds are by looking at their credit ratings. The three biggest rating agencies are Standard & Poor's, Moody's and Fitch. Just as a credit card company might look at your past record of repayments and income to give you a score of credit-worthiness, so rating agencies look at a country's history and future borrowing plans to give it a rating. Big economies like the United States, Germany and Britain have the highest rating – triple A – because it is assumed there is little chance they will not be able to repay their debts.

Explaining debt ratings

RATING	WHAT THAT MEANS
AAA	Highest rating given to countries like US, almost no chance of default
AA	Very strong ability to meet any financial commitments
A	Good ability to meet commitments but could be affected by shocks

RATING	WHAT THAT MEANS
BBB	Adequate ability to meet commitments but bad economic conditions could become a problem
BBB–	Slightly more susceptible to bad economic conditions, the lowest investment grade rating which is the minimum that banks can invest in
BB+	Fine in the near-term but longer term issues could make it susceptible to bad economic conditions
B	More vulnerable to bad economic conditions but currently can repay obligations
CCC	Currently vulnerable and dependent on favourable economic conditions
CC	Highly vulnerable
C	Very highly vulnerable
D	Default

SOVEREIGN DEFAULTS

But what happens if a country can't pay? This is known as a sovereign default. While there are no courts that can chase a country for its debt, sovereign defaulters will likely find it hard to raise any new finance.

Sovereign defaults can also have big implications for international financial markets and policymakers are anxious to avoid domino effects where one country going bankrupt can trigger a chain reaction that triggers a wave of selling and losses.

What usually happens is that the International Monetary Fund assists in restructuring a country's debt so that bondholders get at least something back. For example, Argentina defaulted on its debt in 2002 and came up with a plan to swap $95 billion worth of government bonds paying 15% interest for longer-term securities paying much less.

In early 2010, there was a lot of concern that Greece would be unable to meet its debt obligations. Panic spread through financial markets as any default would hit banks holding Greek debt hard and the crisis started spreading through the euro area. As a result European governments clubbed together to produce a bailout fund for Greece in an attempt to stave off any default.

The panic served as a reminder to governments that they can't go on running up deficits indefinitely. At some point, markets will start demanding the money is paid back if it appears that a country's public finances are on an unsustainable path. This just goes to show how important it is for governments to balance decisions on how much they want to spend against how much they can raise in tax.

WHAT YOU NEED TO READ

▶ The Institute of Fiscal Studies has an excellent website which provides analysis and details of fiscal policy in the UK: *www.ifs.org.uk/*.

▶ For a look at what is happening in the United States, try the Congressional Budget Office website *www.cbo.gov/*.

▶ There is a history and explanation of the budget process in which the government sets fiscal policy in the UK available on the Treasury's website at *www.hm-treasury.gov.uk/ about_budget.htm*.

▶ A good book on how deficits and debt can affect economic growth is *This Time Is Different: Eight Centuries of Financial Folly* by Carmen M. Reinhart & Kenneth S. Rogoff, Princeton University Press, 2010.

▶ For what is probably the definitive story of economist John Maynard Keynes's life and thinking, have a look at the abridged version of Robert Skidelsky's biography *John Maynard Keynes: 1883–1946: Economist, Philosopher, Statesman*, Pan Abridged Edition, 2004.

IF YOU ONLY REMEMBER ONE THING

Governments collect money through taxes and spend it on goods & services like roads and police forces. The difference between what the government collects and spends is the budget balance. Any shortfall is called a deficit and has to be financed through borrowing.

WHAT IT'S ALL ABOUT

- ▶ Types of property and how we measure house prices
- ▶ What factors influence the price of housing
- ▶ How we judge whether houses are affordable
- ▶ Why an investor might buy housing
- ▶ What impact housing has on the wider economy
- ▶ Why house price bubbles might occur

THE MARKET FOR HOUSING

Standard economics textbooks don't often contain a chapter about housing. However, the housing market can have such a substantial impact on the wider economy (and the other way round, for that matter) that it is an essential topic to cover. After all, booms and busts in the housing market have been associated with expansions and recessions in the economy as a whole on many occasions in the past. And, more recently, it was the bust in the US housing market from 2006 onwards that led to the sub-prime crisis, which went on to develop into the biggest financial meltdown for a generation.

Before we get into the nitty gritty of how the housing market works, let's explore a few basic facts about property – or real estate as it is sometimes called. We can break the market down into two major types. First, commercial properties are those that retailers or producers require as a base to sell or produce their goods & services. Think of a High Street store, a manufacturing plant, or an office which houses a call centre.

Second there is the market for residential properties, which will be the focus of this chapter. These are the flats and houses that we see for sale or rent in estate agents' windows and on their websites. They can be freehold, where the land on which the property stands is owned, or leasehold where the land is effectively rented by

The market for real estate

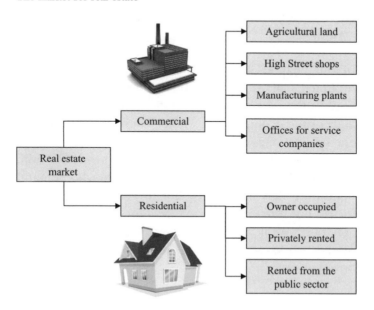

the property owner. Just as with commercial properties, residential real estate can be purchased outright or with a loan – or mortgage. The owner of the property can live in it themselves (known as 'owner occupation'), or alternatively the owner might be a landlord who lets his property out to someone who wants to rent it.

Landlords need not just be private individuals – tenants often rent their homes from private property companies or sometimes from the public sector. Whether a home is owner occupied or rented out is called the 'tenure' of the property. The chart below shows how rates of owner occupation can vary significantly across different countries.

In this chapter we'll be looking mainly at the owner occupied market, as large fluctuations in house prices have in the past impacted significantly on the perform-ance of the economy as a whole. There are many differ-ent sub-markets within owner occupation – the sort of people who demand detached country properties will, for example, be very different from those who demand penthouse flats in the city. But to keep it simple we'll focus on the overall market for property more generally. We'll also get a flavour of how the rental market works as well when we take a closer look at buying-to-let.

Owner occupation rates in Europe

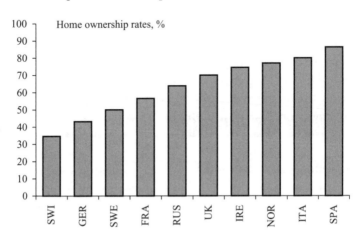

WHO SAID IT

"It's tangible, it's solid, it's beautiful. It's artistic, from my standpoint, and I just love real estate."
– Donald Trump

Housing is an asset in the same way that money is. While it may be more illiquid than money (it is more difficult to convert into a medium of exchange) it is a store of value and it can be used as an investment, as we will see later in the chapter. From this point on we'll refer to 'house prices' as the price of residential property in general – covering all types of owner occupied dwelling (flats and houses alike).

HOW WE MEASURE HOUSE PRICES

In developed economies there tends to be much focus on house prices. It is the topic of many a dinner conversation: everyone seems to have a view on how house prices might or might not move in the future. In some countries the fascination is greater than in others. Take the UK for example. Here's an amazing statistic – on average, two measures of house prices are published every week of the year. That's how much people like to focus on how the price of their most valuable asset – the property they own – changes.

Usually house prices are published on a monthly basis, sometimes in value terms (for example the average price of a house in pounds sterling in the UK, US dollars in America, or euros in continental Europe) and sometimes as an index (prices being set to 100 in some base year). But this is not typically what you'll hear quoted in the media – the biggest focus is how much house prices have changed either over the past month or the past year, normally expressed as a percentage rise or fall.

Just like economic activity, we usually adjust house prices for the ups and downs caused by the time of the year. After all, we wouldn't want to misinterpret a decline in prices during a typically quite month as an *underlying* fall in property prices. For example, house prices might typically rise by more in the first half of the year, and often fall in the second half – which is why it's important to seasonally adjust to smooth out these monthly variations.

A bigger issue relates to the mix of properties sold in any one period. Imagine, for example, that in one month there are lots of small flats sold, but in the next month sales are dominated by large detached houses. Of course,

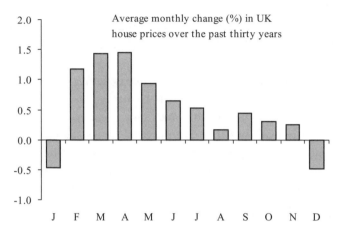

The importance of adjusting house prices for the time of year

Average monthly change (%) in UK
house prices over the past thirty years

prices will go up because the type of house being sold in the second month is larger than in the first. But what we really want to know is whether *the same type of houses or flats* are going up in price – we don't want our house price indicators to be influenced by the sort of properties being sold.

That is why most measures of house prices try to take account of the changing type of house being bought and sold in each period. There are two main ways to do this. The first is by using a statistical adjustment procedure known as 'mix adjustment'. This is where we adjust the price for the size of house being traded, as well as other factors like the location it's in and the facilities that it has. In short, we are trying to make the houses traded in

251

one period comparable with those traded in the next. This is the way that two of the most popular measures of house prices in the UK are calculated – those of the Nationwide building society and the Halifax.

The second way to make sure we are isolating only under-lying moves in house prices is to survey the *same house* every time it comes up for sale. This is called the 'repeat sales' method, but it is complicated by the fact that the same house doesn't often come up for sale. This is the methodology of the most popular house price measure in the US – the Case-Shiller index, named after its developers Karl Case and Robert Shiller.

House price measures don't always tell the same story. Sometimes, they can move in different directions from one another, one rising and another falling *in the same month*. There are a few reasons that this can happen. First, some measures may be biased towards certain regions or towards different types of property (for example cheap flats versus expensive detached houses), which may rise and fall at different rates. Some measures even exclude certain transactions if they are for too high a price, as they may end up distorting the index.

Second, and perhaps more importantly, prices can be measured at *different points in the transaction*. For example, some indicators are designed to measure asking prices – the prices that properties are put on the market for (which, after a good deal of haggling, need not be the same price for which they are finally sold). That's clearly quite early on in the sales process. A little further down the line are prices measured at the time the buyer gets a mortgage approved on the property they intend to buy – at which point they have probably broadly agreed the price at which the property will eventually be sold. And further along the sales process still we can measure prices at the time the house is finally transacted and the keys exchanged.

Whatever stage in the process, when you hear about house prices on the news or in the papers they will almost always be referring to the cash (or what is called the 'nominal') price. But it is often a good idea to adjust this for inflation in the economy. So, if house prices were rising at 10% and inflation was 4%, for example, then 'real' house prices (the rise over and above the rate of inflation) would be 6%. This gives us a better idea of how house prices are changing compared to the underlying rate of prices generally in the economy.

WHAT DRIVES THE PRICE OF HOUSES?

If you've already read the rest of this book then this should come as no surprise: the price of housing is generally determined by the interaction of the demand for and supply of properties. When demand is high sellers know they can get a good price for their property and will often hold out until a buyer comes along who is willing to pay more. Likewise, when there are a lot of new properties coming on to the market it may be more difficult to find buyers for them all, and discounts may be needed to entice potential buyers to part with their money.

In reality when we see house prices changing it's not always clear whether it's the price of the land that's changing or rather the price of the bricks and mortar standing on that land. In most cases the two are usually inseparable. But because building materials don't typically change in price as much as houses do we can probably safely assume that house price movements are more to do with the land that properties occupy than the properties themselves.

To begin with let's have a think about the sort of factors that influence the *demand* for housing:

- ▶ *Mortgage rates.* Most people need a mortgage loan to buy a house, and the higher the cost of borrowing that money (that is, the interest rate) the fewer the number of potential house buyers there are likely to be.
- ▶ *Credit availability.* It is not just the cost of borrowing money that will be important but its availability too. If banks are strapped for cash and are finding it difficult to lend – as was the case in the recent credit crisis – then this could in turn limit the demand for housing.
- ▶ *Household incomes.* A house or flat is often the biggest purchase that a household will make in their lifetime. The size of house they can afford

to buy will depend on their earnings – both now and in the future. Across the economy as a whole household earnings will depend on the total number of people in employment.

▶ *Demographics.* Growth in the population and changes in its composition – in particular the number of people who are in prime 'house buying' age groups – will be important in affecting the total demand for property in an economy. An ageing population in many developed countries over the coming decades may limit the demand for housing in the future, but inward migration in some countries and increased longevity could support housing demand.

▶ *Expectations and confidence.* A person may be less inclined to buy a house when they think prices might fall in the future, but more likely to buy when they believe prices will rise. This is why up and down cycles in housing can so often be self-reinforcing.

▶ *Taxation.* Some tax systems encourage the purchase of housing, others do not. Changes in the tax regime can be important especially for those considering buying a property as an investment as second homes usually attract capital gains tax when they are sold.

▶ *The currency.* If the currency is weak it may encourage buyers from abroad into the market because it will make house prices in that country look cheaper.

▶ *The rate of inflation.* The rate of general price inflation can have an important effect on housing demand. Higher inflation not only tends to push up interest rates, but it also raises in the early years of the mortgage loan the amount that a house buyer must repay relative to their income. This is called the 'front-loading' or 'tilt' effect, and is shown in the chart below. As you can imagine, higher inflation makes it more difficult for a household reliant on borrowing money to buy a house to get on to the housing ladder.

The price of housing too will influence the demand for housing – as the downward sloping line in the graph

The effect of inflation on mortgage payments

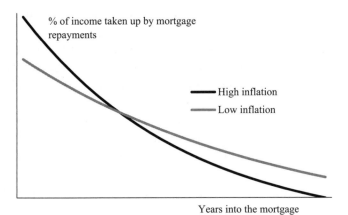

below shows, the higher house prices are, the fewer of them people typically want to buy.

What about the supply of houses? Over short periods of time supply depends on how many people want to sell their houses. But in the long run it will depend on how many houses there are in the country. And, as you can imagine, it's not easy to change this quickly – the stock of owner occupied houses and new house building therefore cannot move around that much in response to changes in house prices. This is why we've drawn a steep line to represent housing supply in the graph below. Developers will be encouraged to build more houses to sell when the price of them rises, but planning regulations and the physical availability of land might prevent them from doing so that easily. We describe supply as

The demand for and supply of houses

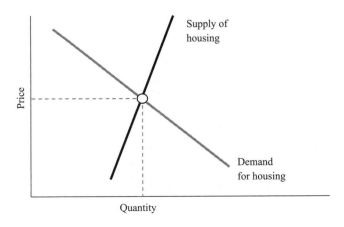

being relatively 'inelastic' when it comes to how it responds to price changes.

The point at which the buyers and sellers are both happy and willing to transact is shown where the demand and supply lines cross in the graph above. Bubbles often develop in the prices of assets such as housing (as they do in other assets like shares and currencies) as people get carried away and begin to believe that prices should be higher than is actually justifiable. Expectations of future capital gains push the demand curve ever higher.

WHO YOU NEED TO KNOW
David Hendry

David Hendry is a British economist who specialises in using statistics to explain economic relationships – an area called econometrics. He was an early user of such techniques to explain how demand and supply in the housing market interact to determine house prices. Almost 30 years ago he wrote a key paper which is still cited by economists forecasting the housing market today (entitled *Econometric modelling of house prices in the United Kingdom*).

Econometrics plays an important role in the lives of economists, allowing us to quantify how important the link is between one economic variable and others. For example, imagine we wanted to establish the impact that household incomes versus interest rates had in influencing house prices. We could do this by using an econometric technique called 'regression analysis', which could tell us both how strong the relationships are and how much we could rely on incomes and interest rates (in this case) to forecast house prices in the future.

We can use econometric techniques to look at house prices across regions (cross section analysis) or over time (time series) – Professor Hendry specialises in time series econometrics. This is a complicated area, not least because lots of economic variables go up over time, raising the risk that when we find a relationship between two or more indicators it may be spurious (for example, house prices and global temperatures may both rise over time, but that does not mean one leads to the other).

259

And because the supply response can be relatively static, it tends to be shifts in demand like this that cause house prices to move.

AFFORDABILITY

One way in which economists like to judge whether the markets have got it right – that is, whether the price of housing is appropriate or not, or whether we're in bubble territory – is to look at measures of housing affordability. The concept is relatively straightforward – for a typical buyer how financially comfortable would it be for them to buy a property with house prices where they are right now? There is no one 'right' measure of affordability, so let's take a look at two of the most commonly used measures along with their advantages and pitfalls.

Firstly, we can look at the average house price and compare it to the income that a typical household brings home after tax. This gives us our first measure of affordability – the **house price-to-income ratio**. Another way of understanding this is that it is the number of years' take home pay that a household needs to earn in order to buy a house. Imagine this ratio was 4, for example – this would mean that a household would have to save every penny of their take home pay for the next four years in order to buy a house outright at current prices.

The reason this is such a closely watched measure of affordability is that banks often restrict the size of mortgage they are willing to lend to households by looking at their incomes. So, the higher are house prices relative to incomes, the more difficult it will be to get a mortgage. Banks also specify the maximum mortgage they are willing to lend as a percentage of the value of the house. So, for example, a bank may not allow people to borrow more than 75% of the value of the house – or another way of putting it is that the bank requires the house buyer to stump up a 25% deposit.

Why do banks limit loans relative to incomes? Well, because the interest payments on the loan will be made out of household income, banks need to be sure the household is earning enough to be able to pay it back – along with the original loan itself. As for limiting the size of the loan relative to the value of the house, this is done to guard against something economists call 'moral hazard' remember we came across this concept in Chapter 6 on central banking. By putting up a decent deposit it ensures that the house buyer has a vested interest in the house – and in repaying the mortgage loan to the bank. Mortgages which are high relative to either incomes or the value of the property are inherently more risky for the bank to lend, so they tend to attract a higher rate of interest for the borrower.

There is a problem with looking at house prices relative to income when trying to judge affordability. While it is helpful in telling us how high house prices look to a potential buyer, it does not tell us what they can afford to pay in mortgage interest payments on an ongoing basis. The reason is that the house price-to-income

The recapitalisation effect

	First period	Second period
House price	£200,000	£400,000
Income	£50,000	£50,000
House price-to-income ratio	**4.0**	**8.0**
Mortgage	£150,000	£300,000
Deposit	£50,000	£100,000
Interest rate	5.0%	2.5%
Interest-only repayment	£7,500	£7,500
Repayment-to-income ratio	**15.0%**	**15.0%**

ratio takes no account of the level of interest rates. What might look a reasonable multiple at one rate of interest may look highly unaffordable when interest rates rise. So another measure of affordability is the 'mortgage repayment-to-income ratio'.

Interest rates have changed a lot over the past few decades. In real terms (in other words, after we adjust for the rate of general price inflation) mortgage interest rates have been falling in developed economies over the past 20 years, making it easier for people to afford more expensive houses relative to their income. In other words, the sustainable or equilibrium house price-to-income ratio should be higher when interest rates fall to permanently lower levels.

Let's illustrate this with an example. Take a look at the chart above. Here we've assumed that in the first period a household with an income of £50,000 per year buys a house worth £200,000 with a 75% mortgage (and therefore a 25% deposit). That means the house price-to-income multiple is 4 (£200,000 divided by £50,000). In the first period we've set interest rates to 5% – which means that the household would be paying £7,500 per year in interest to the bank (that is, 5% of the £150,000 mortgage). The mortgage repayment-to-income ratio would be 15%.

Now imagine that interest rates suddenly halve, from 5% to 2.5%. This makes housing much more affordable for mortgage borrowers. One question we can ask is this – how much could house prices go up in the lower interest rate environment of the second period so that the repayment-to-income multiple remains the same? It turns out that when interest rates halve house prices (and the price-to-income ratio) can double without leading to any worsening in affordability on the repayment-to-income ratio.

Falling UK real mortgage rates over the past 20 years

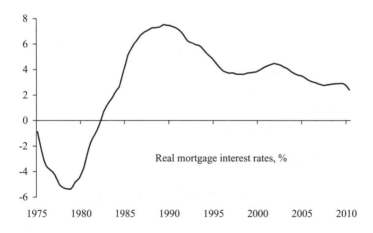

Real mortgage interest rates, %

And this is what actually happened to many housing markets during the 1990s and 2000s. Real interest rates fell (see the previous graph) which then pushed up the sustainable level of house prices relative to incomes. This phenomenon – the impact of lower interest rates being felt through higher house prices – has been termed the 'recapitalisation effect'. Of course, if it turns out that lower real interest rates are not here to stay and they rise sharply in the future, then the recapitalisation effect could work in reverse – higher rates would mean the sustainable level of house prices should be lower.

HOUSING AS AN INVESTMENT

Not everyone buys a property to live in. Some people buy houses as an investment, in the hope that the rise in the value of the house along with the rent they receive from the tenants will together more than pay the interest on the mortgage taken out to buy the property. The purchase of a house in order to let it out is known as 'buy-to-let'. Not all property owners who let out their houses are landlords by choice. Some are what have become known as 'accidental landlords' – they have decided to move house but have not been able to sell their own, and instead opted to let it out.

The UK provides an interesting example here, with buy-to-let schemes heavily promoted from the late-1990s/

early-2000s. Banks and other finance providers offered budding landlords special buy-to-let mortgages, which were plentiful during this period of financial excess. Reflecting the fact they were operating as a business and the higher risks involved, these loans were generally at a higher interest rate and had more stringent terms than if the loan was for an owner-occupier buying a property. But the scheme generally led to lower interest rates than would have been the case otherwise.

The point of the scheme originally was to support the private rental market which had been in long-term decline. But it also led to a surge in demand for private properties, which were taken out of the owner occupied market and offered for rent by buy-to-let landlords. The dramatic rise in property prices in the UK between the mid-1990s and the onset of the credit crisis in 2007 was undoubtedly supported by this scheme. This happened as part of a more general phenomenon globally, as investors faced with low returns elsewhere (shares and interest rates) looked for new opportunities to invest their money. This was dubbed the 'search for yield', with investors often taking on additional risk in order to generate better returns in a period of generally low interest rates.

This brings us on to a third measure of affordability, one which is particularly useful for investors when deciding if it's a good idea to buy and let a property. That is the **rental yield** – how much rent the property generates per year compared to the price the investor has to pay for it.

Take a flat which costs £200,000 – if the investor can get an annual rent of £10,000 for it, then his or her rental yield would be 5%.

But that's in *gross* terms – in other words, it's the percentage return that an investor would receive if there were no deductions. In reality, however, there are estate agents' fees, service charges, taxes, the cost of keeping things in order for the tenant and fallow periods – times when it is not possible to find someone to rent the property. After accounting for all of these costs the return the landlord gets will be lower – we call this the *net* return (as it is net of all the costs). Along with expectations of how much house prices will rise in the future, it is this that the landlord must compare with the cost of owning the flat – either the mortgage rate on the loan taken out to buy it, or the alternative return that could have been earned by investing money elsewhere (remember from Chapter 5 that this is called the opportunity cost). If the combined expected capital and rental return is sufficiently greater – to compensate for the risks involved – than the cost of financing the property then it makes sense to buy-to-let.

This way of assessing affordability has its roots in asset pricing theory. Think about when you buy a share in a company – what influences how much you are willing to pay for it is how much of a dividend will be paid to you each year for holding the share, and also how much you think the share will rise in value in the future. A housing market investor thinks of the price of property in the

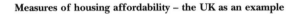

Measures of housing affordability – the UK as an example

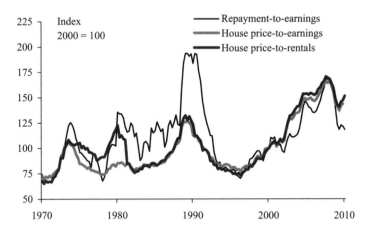

same way as a stock market investor thinks about the price of shares, viewing the rental payments in the same way as dividends.

THE IMPORTANCE OF HOUSING TO THE WIDER ECONOMY

One of the reasons economists spend so much time analysing the housing market is because of the impact that it can have on the wider economy. Developments in the housing market can affect the rate at which the economy grows, the rate of inflation in the economy and, as a result, the rate of interest that the central bank sets.

The first point to make is that the relationship between the housing market and the economy generally can vary substantially both across countries and over time. Take a look at the chart below. This shows, for the US and the UK, the relationship between house price growth and the growth rate of household spending in the economy (both adjusted for inflation) over a long period of time – 100% indicates a perfect positive relationship between the two (in other words both go up and down at the same time) whereas zero would suggest there is no relationship. As you can see, spending and house prices tend to move strongly in the same direction as each other.

The relationship between house prices and consumer spending

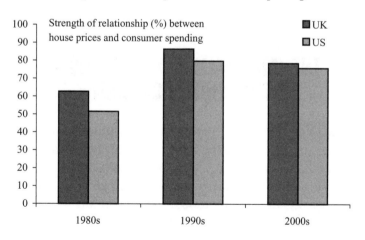

Why is there such a strong relationship between house prices and spending (and thereby economic) growth, and is it reasonable to conclude that it is the housing market that drives the economy or is it the other way round?

The theory that housing influences the economy usually relies on a phenomenon called 'wealth effects'. When house prices rise, people who own property feel wealthier since the price of their most valuable asset has gone up. People may feel more confident about the state of the economy and job prospects, which in turn encourages them to go out and spend. Moreover, housing is usually an important part of one's savings – it is an asset that can be liquidated in retirement, perhaps by downscaling to a smaller house and using the proceeds to spend. If house prices rise, therefore, there is less of a need to save now for retirement. And, for any given amount of income you earn, the less you save the more you spend.

There are also more direct links between house prices and spending in the economy than wealth effects. If a household needs money to spend but would prefer not to have to pay the high rates associated with a personal loan, one option would be to borrow against the equity in their house – or 'equity withdrawal' as it is known. Secured borrowing (such as mortgage loans, where failure to repay can mean losing the house) is usually done at much lower interest rates than unsecured borrowing (where there is no asset for the bank to take in the event of a default). When house prices rise, there is more opportunity to borrow against the equity that has built up in the asset.

Let's go back to the example we looked at earlier, where a person owns a house worth £200,000 but also has a mortgage of £150,000. Banks these days don't usually like offering loans worth more than 75% of the value of the house, so if the house price stays at £200,000 the owner would find it difficult to borrow any more against their house. But imagine if the house price were to jump to £250,000. If the bank were to lend up to its 75% limit that would mean the owner could borrow an extra £37,500 – 75% of the increase in the value of the property. They could then use that to spend, which would raise the rate of economic growth. In other words, higher house prices make it easier for homeowners to access credit from the bank.

Another reason to think that higher housing transactions (and in turn higher house prices) should raise the rate of consumer spending is that when people move they tend to spend money on consumer durable goods – such as kitchen equipment, carpets, curtains and televisions. However, it could be that these purchases are simply being brought forward to be timed to coincide with the house purchase, so greater spending on household goods now could mean less spending in the future.

But, there are also some arguments to suggest that developments in the housing market do not *cause* but are simply *associated with* changes in the state of the economy. We've already seen that consumer spending and house prices are closely related, but it could be that both housing and spending are influenced by movements in the same things – in particular, household incomes and interest rates. A rise in incomes or a fall in interest rates, for example, would support consumer spending and housing demand at the same time without one *leading to* changes in the other.

Another reason to question the relationship between house prices and consumption is that when house prices go up, if you move house then you will only have to pay an equivalently higher price for another house. And think of the people who will be out of pocket who are buying housing for the first time – surely their spending will go down as prices increase? After all, they will need to take on a larger mortgage to buy property when prices rise, which also means increased interest costs. That could eat into their disposable income and reduce how much they have left to spend on other things.

Higher house prices are simply a transfer of wealth from those who don't own property to those who do. Rising prices should not be considered to be productive in any sense, therefore, apart from the increased provision of estate agent and legal services that are typically associated with more housing transactions and thereby higher house prices.

BUBBLE TROUBLE AND THE SUB-PRIME CRISIS

Because of the importance of the housing market when things go wrong there are typically significant negative knock-on effects throughout the rest of the economy. In an upswing house prices can be driven higher by expectations of future capital gains, but they can end up going too far – just like they did in the run up to the sub-prime crisis. We learnt about the sub-prime crisis in Chapter 3 – people who weren't in a financial position to be owner occupiers nonetheless borrowed money and bought houses.

The concept of fair value or the equilibrium price simply got lost in the hubris as buyers jumped on the band-wagon of ever rising prices. But eventually the laws of economics suggest that prices will eventually head back to where the fundamental drivers of demand and supply tell us they should be. And that is exactly what happened during the crisis – house prices in America began to fall from late 2006.

Recessions and house price corrections often go hand in hand, which can be bad news for home owners – especially if they borrowed too much to buy their house in the first place. When a buyer has a large mortgage relative to the price of the house, it does not take much of a decline in house prices before how much they owe becomes larger than the value of the house – so called

WHO YOU NEED TO KNOW
Robert Shiller

Robert Shiller has spent much of his academic
life studying bubbles – or unsustainable booms –
in asset prices, in particular stocks & shares
and house prices. He is responsible, along
with Karl Case, for developing the most widely
watched house price index in America –
the Case-Shiller index, which measures house
price inflation by looking at repeat sales of
the same houses.

Perhaps his best known book is *Irrational
Exuberance*, named after a phrase originally
coined by Alan Greenspan in 1996, then
Chairman of the Board of Governors at the
Federal Reserve (America's central bank) to
describe excessive stock market valuations
at the time. When the book was first published
markets were gripped by the dot.com boom –
the surge in the price of shares in internet
companies that was eventually to reverse,
helping bring about the 2001 recession
in the US and noticeable slowdowns in most
developed economies.

The field of economics within which Shiller works is called 'behavioural' economics or finance – an investigation of how households, investors and firms make decisions and what their impact is on the economy. While that might seem to be what most economists do anyway, the important difference is that it questions the assumption of 'rationality' in economics – the idea that individuals will always operate to maximise their own self-interest (a bit like Adam Smith's invisible hand story). It is a direct challenge to the Efficient Markets Hypothesis, which says that in the markets for finance and assets (such as shares and houses) prices are always at the right level because they reflect all information that is known to affect the price. The volatility of asset prices – especially associated with the credit crisis – has increased the level of interest in behavioural economics over recent years.

'negative equity'. And this became a problem for home owners in America in the late 2000s when the recession associated with the credit crisis left many sub-prime borrowers jobless, at which point they could no longer afford to repay the interest on their mortgages.

WHO SAID IT

"As house prices fall, a huge amount of financial folly is being exposed. You only learn who has been swimming naked when the tide goes out."
– **Warren Buffet**

In such situations in the first instance some households might go into arrears, falling behind on their monthly repayments to the bank. Banks usually allow a period of grace before taking action, but if they believe a household will not be able to repay their debt they might move to repossess the property. This means forcing the owners to sell, using the proceeds to pay off the mortgage. With negative equity, of course, this may not be possible.

In most European countries, if the sale price of a house is insufficient to cover the mortgage then the home-owner owes the remainder to their bank. However, in some states of America mortgages are what are known as 'non-recourse' – in the event of a fall in property prices and a forced sale, the homeowner is only liable to pay back the current value of the property, and not the mort-gage. The sub-prime crisis saw home-owners posting their keys back to the bank, as they were unwilling to continue paying interest on a larger mortgage than the declining value of their property.

The big problem with forced sales is that they can end up reinforcing the downturn, as the supply of houses coming on to the market is increased, depressing prices further. And, as we learnt above, the further prices fall the less wealthy people feel – spending in the economy slows, unemployment rises, and the whole process con-tinues. Such a situation often requires outside interven-tion – support from either the government (perhaps a cut in housing taxes) or the central bank (lower interest rates) to stabilise conditions.

The scale of the recent sub-prime crisis was so large that its effects will continue to be felt for many years to come. Only the intervention of policymakers on a grand scale has thus far prevented a repeat of the 1930s Great Depression. The power of the housing market to make and break an economy is truly remarkable.

WHAT YOU NEED TO READ

▶ An excellent article examining the relationship between economic growth and the housing market can be found on the Bank of England's website. See Andrew Benito, Jamie Thompson, Matt Waldron and Rob Wood's article, 'House prices and consumer spending': *www.bankofengland.co.uk/publications/quarterlybulletin/qb060201.pdf*.

▶ A website which posts interesting articles about the UK housing market (and whether house prices are sustainable) is rather aptly called House Price Crash and can be found here: *www.housepricecrash.co.uk/*.

▶ Robert Shiller has written two particularly popular books. In *Irrational Exuberance*, Princeton University Press, 2000 & 2005, he looks at destabilising asset price booms, while in *Animal Spirits* (2009, with George Akerlof) he examines how human psychology can explain the problems of housing market excesses.

▶ A very accessible book which looks at bubbles in financial and asset markets is *The Origin of Financial Crises* by George Cooper, Harriman House, 2008.

▶ Finally, the tutor2u website has a good section on how the housing market works, explaining in particular how the housing market interacts with the wider economy and the importance of demand and supply: *www.tutor2u.net/economics/housingmarket.htm.*

IF YOU ONLY REMEMBER ONE THING

House prices, just like the prices of everyday goods & services, are determined by the interaction of demand and supply. There's more than one way to judge whether house prices are affordable, but prices can – and often do – move a long way from these measures of fair value. House prices can have a serious destabilising effect on economies, both in the upswing and the subsequent downswing.

CONCLUSION

We hope this book has given you everything you need to understand the basic workings of the economy whether you're starting a new job, studying or just plain interested in one of the most fascinating subjects there is today.

The world has changed a lot in the last decade. Just think of the rising economic power of China or India. Or the fact that modern computers and the internet mean that you can access information or services from around the world in seconds.

Despite all the change, the basic laws of economics – like the way supply and demand determine prices – hold true. This book should have given you enough knowledge about the everyday concepts that economists use to apply to just about any situation.

That's not to say economics is immutable. Much more so than in the natural sciences, fashions can change quickly in the application of economic theory. For example, you read how Keynesianism gave way to monetarism which made room for inflation targeting. But the underlying precepts often remain the same.

In the last few years, economists have been struggling with the fallout from the credit crunch and the recession that followed – the worst global downturn since the Great Depression of the 1930s. Before that, they were trying to get their heads around the housing booms in many parts of the world. The two, as we have seen, were inextricably linked – excesses in a boom often lay the groundwork for a subsequent bust.

Each new phase in history provides room for new theories and helps economics advance a little bit more. The coming decades are likely to produce completely new challenges for the science. We can only guess what some of these might be. But questions such as how to deal with ageing populations in developed economies or rapid growth in emerging markets seems a good bet for now.

We hope that this book has shown you that economics can be simple and that it can also be interesting. It should help you to understand some of the biggest issues facing us today and tomorrow and we hope you will be inspired to learn more.

ACKNOWLEDGEMENTS

Many thanks to Ellen Hallsworth (Wiley), Mark Wall (Deutsche Bank), Rajat Goswami and Jean-Christophe Grey for their time, advice and expertise. Of course, we couldn't have written this book without the support of our friends and family. In particular, Kirsty Good, Tamawa Desai and our parents Barbara & Malcolm Montgomery, Ken & Val Buckley and Jyoti & Niranjan Desai deserve a special mention for all their love and patience.

SOURCES

INDEX